Don't Ask, Do Tell!

When I finally told the military
"Kiss my gay ..."

William Bonzo

Don't Ask, Do Tell

"All hands on deck! William has something to say. This is a must read!"

Pete

"I couldn't put it down, and was late for work."

Takahiro

"Bill has a sense of humor that will keep you laughing."

Beverly

"Given how painful some of these memories must be, I'm more than impressed—I'm moved by your courage."

Sarah

"Forget the book, make the movie."

Mark

"I'm glad you had the courage to share your story."

Michele

"The Navy Department trusts that you will continue your interest in the naval service."

Secretary of the Navy

"No, trust **US**!"

William Bonzo

DISCLAIMER

Some names are changed, and others are omitted.

I mean no disrespect towards the United States military, nor towards those who serve or who have served in uniform.

This is my eyewitness account of actual events. However, I hope this book will be read with the understanding that this is my interpretation of the events.

Some would say that hindsight is twenty-twenty; I want the phone number of their Optometrist!

To be sure, it is foresight I hope to improve with my story.

"By being armed, but with no weapons, great battles may be won."

Tao Te Ching

Don't Ask, Do Tell

CONTENTS

"The most excellent Jihad is that for the conquest of self. The ink of the scholar is more holy than the blood of the martyr."

Muhammad

"Let your mind wander in simplicity, blend your spirit with the vastness."

Chuang-tzu

DEDICATION

This book is dedicated to all the servicemen and women who serve their country.

Somewhere in the world, right now, a gay man or lesbian woman is risking his or her life in order that you have the freedom to read this book – a book which you would not be free to read in many places in the world today.

As of the date of this book, over four thousand American soldiers have been killed in the war in Iraq, and over 100,000 have been wounded. The tally in Afghanistan is still mounting.

This book is also dedicated to the family, friends and community who miss them every day.

William Bonzo, LT, SC, USNR

"Let yourself be open, and life will be easier."

Buddah

Don't Ask, Do Tell

INTRODUCTION

The number of U.S. soldiers killed in recent wars is staggering, and the U.S. is still under threat. We need every soldier we have serving in the armed forces.

If the most conservative, homophobic senator were being attacked by an enemy combatant, I would, as a member of the U.S. Armed Services, jump in to protect him – risking my own life in order to save his. That's what I'm trained to do, and that's the commitment I've made. Would the senator refuse my protection in that moment because I'm gay? I doubt it.

Publishing this book, I feel as if I'm peeking furtively through the dark green camouflage of the hedge in front of my quarters, looking left, then right, then quickly left again. The news headlines on Don't Ask, Don't Tell are constantly changing.

Is it time to tell? Is it really safe to come "out" yet?

I think so, I tell myself bravely.

It's been a long time coming.

I've had plenty of reason to hesitate: if I tell, and if the mainstream media pick up the story, how will the current struggle of gays and lesbians serving, be affected?

Will some jerk in Washington wave my book feverishly in the air at a congressional hearing on the never ending debate on allowing gays and lesbians to serve openly, as evidence against our fight for fairness?

Or will a previously homophobic serviceman or woman finish the book, then look up and declare that their ship mate's preferences are not a threat to them, or the unit.

Come along with me, as a new, young, fresh Ensign I participate in some extraordinary events, like the commissioning of the equally new USS *Clifton Sprague* (FFG-16) at the Naval Ship Yard in Bath, Maine.

We'll go to the bank with a brown paper bag from Safeway, wearing jeans and a ski jacket, to get one million dollars for our maiden voyage, instead of **using** the suggested uniform, military van, and armed escort that would only announce, "Hey, I've got a lot of cash here!"

Come along as, before the ink dries on the money and I've learned how to spell "Ensign," I become a veteran on the battle front during the invasion of Grenada—Operation Urgent Fury—where four good men of SEAL team six will be killed the first night out. The heart-pounding air and sea search for them will be to no avail. Our skipper will turn the forty-two hundred ton ship on a dime the instant I report to the bridge that I've seen what appear to be bodies in the water, but which turn out to be only coconuts floating on the surface.

Do keep pace, won't you? We've no time to grieve their loss.

You grab the Dramamine, while I put on the Navy Expeditionary Medal I just earned, and train for my Surface Warfare Qualification by driving a guided missile cruiser with no bloody fin stabilizers across the North Atlantic in a gale storm. We won't get much sleep...

But a flight crew of six men, and a total ship's complement of over two hundred men will have the opportunity to at least lie in their bunks, surviving a potential catastrophe which will be averted when I take action on an in-flight emergency, without hesitation, and earn a nomination as NAVAIRLANT (Navy Air Atlantic) pro of the week!

We survive, obviously, and I get promoted to Lieutenant.

Moving forward without pause you and I will sleep in places we never imagined and be exposed both to nerve gas and new cultures. We'll learn new languages while meeting new people and be shot at and chased by others. Goodness, can't we all just get along?

We'll eat in both regal and rotten places. The reality of death will enface you. But not to worry, I'll be right beside you, watching your back throughout the ride.

As a gay man in the United States Navy, I was *completely* alone, and I even tried to commit suicide. Sure, I had friends but I couldn't *talk* to them. Yes, I had thoughts about sex, but the military operation or mission was paramount. Yes, I "looked." Man or woman, gay or straight, Muslim, Mormon, et al.: we all *look!* Having the courage of conviction, sense of morality, or sense of duty makes all the difference between looking and touching.

Camouflage is used by the military to conceal personnel or equipment from an enemy and make them appear to be part of the natural surroundings. To be sure, there was and still is nothing natural to military minds about gays and lesbians in uniform. Hence, I would excel at camouflage and survive the enemy I served in order to fight the enemies of our country, or so I thought.

Confused about who the real enemy is? Me too! And, voila, that is the microsecond of doubt that can get a person killed in a battle such as the ones to come in the Persian Gulf.

And finally on our journey, after you've thrown up lunch from the ride to date, or was it something you ate along the way, you'll visit me in Christchurch, New Zealand where I am stationed with the National Science Foundation—Operation Deep Freeze—me, without a scientific bone in my body!

New Zealand now has a non-nuclear policy and forbids foreign ships that carry nuclear weapons or are powered by nuclear power from entering their ports. Since the official policy of the United States Navy is neither to confirm nor deny the presence of nuclear weapons on its ships, I enter the country by air and set up camp at Christchurch airport as the Officer in Charge of the U.S. Navy Exchange and Commissary.

McMurdo station in Antarctica is also on our itinerary. Great, I joined the navy to see the world and go to sea, yet I end up on an iceberg!

So, what do you think? Are you up for an adventure? I tell my tales every week in installments to a friend at Gold's Gym SOMA. I always start out by saying, "Did I tell you the story about..." and he is either rapt with attention, nodding sympathetically, or laughing out loud.

He repeatedly says, "This is good *shit*. You should write a book!"

"OK," I respond, "But some might say after reading it that I'm *full of shit*."

To be sure, how this book is perceived, will ultimately depend on your perspective:

Taoism: Shit happens.

Hare Krishna: Shit happens rama ding.

Hinduism: This shit happened before.

Sunni Islam: Shi'ite happens.

Zenoism: What is the sound of shit happening?

Buddhism: When shit happens, is it really shit?

Confucianism: Confucias Say, "Shit happens."

7th Day Adventist: Shit happens on Saturday.

Protestantism: If I work hard shit won't happen.

Catholicism: If shit happens I deserve it.

Judaism: Why does shit always happen to me?

Impressionism: From a distance, shit looks like a garden.

Idolism: Let's bronze this shit.

Capitalism: That's *my* shit.

Communism: It's everybody's shit.

Commercialism: Let's package this shit.

Rastafarianism: Let's smoke this shit!

PROLOGUE

"Bonjour, William" I heard the waiter say from the back of his head, as I entered the familiar Parisian café I had lunched at during the years I was at University. "Soupe a l'oignon, salad d'epinards" I began my order, only to have my sentence completed by Pierre "vin rouge, crème brulee, café – oui, je sais." Am I that predictable, I asked myself while looking towards the shaded, tree lined boulevard.

I had just received a Bachelor's Degree in The General Arts and Sciences. Great, I now knew a little bit about a lot of things, but not a lot about any one thing in particular. Now what the hell was I supposed to do with my life? My father had said get a degree, but was nonspecific. He had paid for my schooling, but with the caveat that once completed I was on my own.

At just that moment, I saw the also now- familiar form of a U.S.Navy recruiter walk past the café, the same handsome man I had wistfully looked at for years. I'm predictable, Pierre? We'll see – "l'addition, s'il vous plait." I exited the café, followed the uniformed man, and joined the Navy, just like that. Free food, free lodging, and lots of exercise – ooh rah!

Don't Ask, Do Tell!

CHAPTER ONE:
CADENCE

"Swing those arms, stay in step, march with the man on your left right left, left, left, left right left."

"That's five left foots" I counted incredulously.

"You want me to fall or what? And by the way, what the hell is a woman, albeit a dyke, doing as my drill sergeant here at Officer Candidate School in bloody freezing Newport, Rhode Island? Is this just her day job?" As our drill sergeant continued to belt out the orders, I continued discussing it with myself. "I wonder if she realizes that I am related to a former president of the United States, and therefore probably exempt from this torture."

"PAPA Company, double-quick time!" she barked. Great, she was trying to kill me. "Three more laps around the parade grounds!" she barked again without interruption. *No thanks, I've seen this view already. Can we hit the gym now?* I asked myself, since she obviously wasn't listening to me. "PAPA Company, halt! Hit the showers!"

Now we're talking. I'd only been on base for one day, and I was about to experience my first awkward moment.

In boot camp, one has only five minutes to shit, shower, and shave. If you take more than five minutes, you don't eat. With all the torture I'd suffered at the direction of the dyke sergeant, I needed food.

The military can force you to be very efficient, so since there were forty of us and only twenty showers, we paired up: two men per stall. I stood in the locker room like a kid in a candy store, unable to choose my shower buddy from the buff and brave before me. And then I saw him: oh, let's just call him Adonis. Sculpted muscles, washboard abs, and a little bit slow off the mark—cute and dumb, thank you, God.

Adonis and I ended up in the last stall. His chest was chiseled, his butt was hard and round, his legs were carved by Michelangelo, and his ... well, never you mind. I saw him first.

For the duration of our basic training, this scene would repeat itself. Thank goodness it was the dead of winter and minus 5 degrees— nothing "grows." I would steal furtive glances, pretending to be looking for the soap, but I knew this was the military, and imposed on myself a policy of don't look, don't touch!

The Mess Hall is where we ate our meals, when on base. In all truthfulness, the military served good chow. The décor, cinder blocks painted grey, long folding tables and non-descript stacking chairs left something to be desired. However, a sense of urgency hung over us as we ate like ravenous farm animals, because it was only 5 a.m. and I doubted our sergeant would return with paint and wall paper samples in order to spend the remainder of the day decorating.

"Jump in!" shouted the now-familiar voice of Satan's sister after we had run from the Mess Hall to the Natatorium, stripped to our skivvies, and stood at formation around the deep end of a very large, formidable-looking swimming pool. Her voice echoed off the walls and water, there now seemingly being a hundred of her shouting at the forty of us.

I looked to my left at Adonis, who now resembled a frightened boy, and said reassuringly, "Hey, I'll be right next to you." For forty-five minutes we had to tread water, with no stopping. None. Ever. The sergeant walked the rim of the pool with a look that said, "If you put your hand on the ledge of the pool, I'll break every bone in it with my boot." Some choice, huh: Broken bones, or drowning.

I love to swim and could stay in the water all day. However, staying close to Adonis, I sensed he wasn't going to make it. I started coaching him. "Float on your back for a while, then turn over and doggie paddle—we're almost there" I said while waving my intact hands gently in the water, keeping myself afloat. It must have been all his solid muscle dragging him under.

Seconds after the final whistle had blown; I wrapped one arm around his massive chest and pulled his exhausted, submerged body to the pool edge with my other arm. Nothing sexual even remotely entered my mind – I was just saving my mate's life.

Apparently we had passed the tread-water test, but now we had to learn how to jump into the pool properly, as if jumping into the ocean from a sinking ship. "Yippee, we're going *back into the water*" I exclaimed with a smile, slapping Adonis on his wet ass, hoping only to knock the fear out of him, while glancing at our dyslexic leader for instructions. "Remove all jewelry," she growled, "as the reflection of sunlight on it will attract sharks." "Now, arms to your side, hold your nose, cross your legs, and jump" she persisted with an evil smile of her own. "She's trying again to make me fall, isn't she?" I said under my breath as I complied with her instructions and soon resembled a pretzel!

I didn't know it at the time, but, this drill would seem like gleeful fun compared to the time years later when I'd have to put these skills to use in a real situation, jumping from a deck of grey steel into the murky green waters of the Persian Gulf, and not clear pool water.

I also didn't know that on that future ship, I would be in charge of the money, and would be instructed to take as much as I could with me in the life boat, along with my cash book of records. I got the cash, but in the fever pitch of the ship sinking I lost the cash book. The crew in my life boat was *very* protective of *me* since I had the *cash* and there was no record of it!

Also as yet unforeseen would be my cousin Captain Hector Bonzo jumping from the deck of the *General Begrano*, an Argentine cruiser that would be sunk in the Falklands war by the British hunter-killer nuclear submarine HMS *Conqueror*. I guess we both paid attention to the abandon ship drill in boot camp, grateful that we weren't among the 323 men who went down with the ship.

But for now, I was still just concerned with getting through basic training. Adonis and I would hang out together, going to the gym in our free time, reclining on his bunk discussing celestial navigation, or getting off base once to have a civilized dinner at the Chart House in Newport.

At the base gym, we were a couple, but not a *couple*. I'd spot him as he bench-pressed 300 pounds, and he'd push me for one last, painful set on my leg presses. The situation was neither awkward, nor suspicious – we were just two guys working out together.

In the privacy and quiet of our barracks, we'd lie close to each other on his rack, me with book in hand, him looking towards the ceiling for the answer to my question from the text on navigation by the stars. When he couldn't find the correct answer I'd punch him on his bicep, regain eye contact with him, and say "No matter, they probably have modern machines on the ships so we won't even need to use a stupid, simple sextant."

Off base, we were a bit more relaxed and loose-tongued. He'd talk about his girlfriend back at home somewhere I had never heard of and I'd talk about, well, not girls but a safe subject such as food. He had grown up herding cattle and shoveling cow dung, and I had grown up watching Julia Child cook, and swimming as often as I could get near a body of water.

Back on base again it had now become a six-month routine of free food, free lodging, lots of exercise, and young, in-shape men—a gay man's menu in heaven! Yet, in retrospect, I had voluntarily entered my prison.

It was voluntary because I wouldn't allow myself to cross that invisible line and actually act on any of my many attractions. I took my military duties seriously, and I promised myself I wasn't going to do anything that could get me kicked out of this new life I'd chosen.

One that had everything I wanted, but the one thing I needed and wasn't allowed to have – a *real relationship*.

"Muffle it, you idiot...before Quasimodo bounds over here and reassigns you to an iceberg in Antarctica!"

Don't Ask, Do Tell

CHAPTER TWO:
GRADUATION

"Ensign Bonzo!" screamed the Master Chief; "care to join the class?" as the monotony of class work at Officer Candidate School went on and on and on. *No, not really. I was napping.* I bolted to attention, having been so rudely awoken. Celestial Navigation is b-o-r-i-n-g, and we've been in this stultifying classroom since 8 a.m.

"Let's go outside and play," I suggested though telepathy, while also glancing towards the window, *"maybe run around the Parade Grounds a few more times..."*

"Ensign Bonzo!" he persisted. I pounded my head on the desk several times, indicating that I thought the Master Chief was oppressive and boorish, then looked right at him and suggested that he just needed a hug, which earned me a trip to the Principal's office. Well, actually the Sergeant's quarters where she said "Close the door, Ensign Bonzo."

Believe it or not, Satan's sister and I had a civilized chat! We talked about everything except the military! She never mentioned a husband, or even a male companion, but often referred to her "friend." I was looking at her with bewilderment, analyzing whether it was a trap or just two kindred souls bonding.

After all, she was keenly aware that Adonis and I had become inseparable, both on and off base.

While she had done most of the talking, I did volunteer that I considered it my duty to help my mate survive boot camp, and that his two weaknesses, class work and swimming, were my strengths. I omitted the part about my cooking skills, for fear of hearing an "Ah hah! I knew it."

Having passed the first of what would become over the course of my military career innumerable manhood tests, I was allowed to go back to play with the other boys.

I'll show her who the man is, I told myself decidedly. I volunteered for anything and everything that Rambo himself could do. Others with a similar testosterone rush earned a Marksman rating with small caliber weapons – I excelled to the highest rating of Expert! Others with need of manhood qualification could run an eight minute mile – I did it in six! And I never mentioned Bananas Foster or quails flambéed with Cognac (yum) again – not even to Adonis.

Which brings me closer to graduation day some months later; I had successfully proven I was a man and all that class work seemed like a megillah.

I had continued my fruitless attempts to communicate with the Master Chief with only a fixed stare which he mistook for me sleeping with my eyes open, and not telepathy.

None the less, all the stuff he was putting into my brain might be useful, one day, if I decided to write a book about the prison, I projected, turning my gaze again to the window, and what would very soon lie beyond it.

Our last day at boot camp: ooh rah! And my cellmate, not to be confused with my shower buddy Adonis, was still a moron! He couldn't even make his rack properly after six months of practice. "When Martha Stewart inspects our room, your bed sheets need to be so taught that the quarter she will purposefully drop on your rack, has to bounce off the sheets," I explained with broad strokes of my hands, at the same time smiling to myself at his failure to get the Martha Stewart/our Sergeant double entendre. "Even Nelson Mandela knows how to make his own bed in prison," I continued loudly for emphasis.

Finally at the graduation ceremony, when we got out first duty assignments, I heard the Master Chief scream the moron's name.

"Ensign Avery!" (Do we still have an anger issue here, I wondered disappointedly?)

"Avery- I," responded butthead.

"You have been assigned as the navigator on the nuclear submarine *Memphis*."

"God," I thought, "the world as we know it is over when he steers that thing into a collision course with the East Coast."

"Ensign Bonzo!" screamed the Master Chief.

Now, understand that in the military, when a superior, or higher ranking, individual calls your name, expecting a response, such as in roll call, you are to respond by saying your last name, plus "I." This tried-and-true military tradition I was happy to embrace.

"Bon-zai," I screamed right back. Within a microsecond the overweight, hairy, Hunchback of Notre Dame look-alike Master Chief with severe halitosis crossed the vast assembly hall and was poised a quarter of an inch away from my face.

"You think that's funny? Do you know how many men died defending this country from those little slant-eyed yellow bastards?" he spat at me as his round face became red on a field of white that was his uniform.

"Four thousand fifty-seven dead, 1,021 wounded?" I guessed sarcastically in response to his rhetorical question.

"Give me fifty!" he screamed. Great, I love exercise and dropped to the floor to give him his fifty push-ups. As I was enjoying the workout, I was also thinking that perhaps my French accent could be used to blame the faux-pas, as the liaison of the zo and the following

I become *Zai* in French. "No doubt you just misunderstood me," I'll say when I tutor him shortly.

"Forty-eight, forty-nine, fifty," I finished counting off the push-ups.

"One, two, three," I started counting off fifty more push-ups, moments after his French lesson…

And so, graduation day continued in alphabetical order; all those with last names ending in *A-P* in one line then *Q-Z* in a second line opposite and in direct line of sight of the first. I was opposite and facing Ensign Nicolas Xenos, Papa Company's class clown and voted most likely to be queer. When the roll call and duty assignments finally got down to him, he winked at me and blew me a kiss!

Uncontrollable laughter sputtered from my lips, then full force from my diaphragm. "Muffle it, you idiot," I tried telling myself, "Before Quasimodo bounds over here and reassigns you to an iceberg in Antarctica!" Demonstrating initiative that later in my career would earn me the Navy Achievement Medal, I voluntarily dropped to the deck and began counting yet again.

Antarctica, on average, is the coldest, driest, and windiest continent on the planet, I remembered from class while counting. But was the Master Chief aware of this? I looked quickly in his direction and awaited his imminent arrival above me. There are no permanent human residents, yet, I recalled, bracing for his words. "Only cold-adapted plants and animals survive in Antarctica," he spat at me in a threatening tone.

Would I be destined for the same fate as the doomed 1912 expedition to that frozen continent? Little did I know at the time, but my future would indeed hold earning a Navy Expeditionary Medal.

But, at this point in my career I was happy enough to have met, befriended, tutored and saved from drowning Adonis, and winning the popular vote for Papa Company's Mr. Congeniality!

"Do we get to eat before we leave base for the last time?" I shot a final jab at the Master Chief, as I walked across the parade grounds and out the gate without looking back.

Although I would never see Adonis again, I think of him often, smiling—and I'm always hoping he finally learned to swim!

"I may be tempted to act on the feelings I've had since puberty."

CHAPTER THREE:
CAN I REALLY DO THIS?

Having survived boot camp and basic training, I had learned that my first duty assignment would be in beautiful, bloody freezing Bath, Maine! It may as well have been Antarctica.

OK, take a deep breath I told myself while sitting alone this time at the Chart House in Newport. No one at boot camp figured out I was queer – au contraire, they thought I was Rambo! I missed Adonis…

I had seven days to complete my PCS (permanent change of station) orders, and get the short distance from Newport, Rhode Island to Maine. Going to New York appealed to me, as I could have run around Central Park – I liked running! But, in that big city I knew I may have been tempted to act on the feelings I'd had since puberty, yet to date had never acted on. It's easy to hide in a crowd I tried convincing myself. No, no…I was in the military now; just bury those thoughts in the same place as Jimmy Hoffa.

So instead, I just crossed the bridge to Narragansett, to visit my cousin Lieutenant Commander Carter, and his god-fearing family. That would keep me on the "straight" and narrow, for now…

Arriving at their average ranch house, on an average cull-de-sac, in an average New England town I had mixed feelings. No one in my family knew I was gay, and if they had I would probably have been booted out of both the family and the military!

My cousin Ed Carter was a US Navy helicopter pilot when on active duty, and now a Rhode Island State Trooper. He had a wife, three kids, and a dog – it didn't get any more average than this. What's more, they went to church – twice a week. What was I thinking when I decided to stop here? I may as well have stopped in Mayberry, USA.

Still, they were family, and with the loss of my buddy Adonis I needed familiar faces around me. My cousin Dianne was always happy when I'd visit them, because I cooked, and she got a break. That fact, plus the lack of any girlfriend talk on my part should have been their first and second clues as to my *preferences*. But hey, I was in the military, and went to church with them, so I couldn't possibly be queer. I talked to them over dinner about boot camp, and my friend Adonis whose life I had saved. They nodded approvingly, and indicated during mouthfuls of Coq au Vin that they were glad I was making friends.

It wasn't that I didn't like seeing them; they were perfectly nice people, and they were extended family. But while serving them slices of a caramel flan, I was critically aware of how little they knew about me, about my secret, true self.

My Aunt Ruth and Uncle Dale had also stopped here on their way down from our cottage in Ontario, Canada. I had loved spending summers by the lake in Canada when I was younger, reading for my American cousins all the canned goods that were printed in French, and always chopped enough firewood to heat all of Toronto!

One night at our log cabin, I was freezing my ass off so tip-toed towards the stone fireplace to light a fire. My aunt said "William?" Opening the door to their bedroom, I was hit by a blast of cold artic air, her lying practically naked in bed, no covers, and the window open; my uncle next to her, had on several layers of woolen clothing, and was buried under the covers. "Oui?" I said innocently, to which she replied "Don't you light that fire!"

"Coffee, anyone?" I said returning to Mayberry from my reminiscence, as the ladies cleared the table while the men moved to the lounge to watch sports. I stood in the doorway, debating which way I should go, while thinking that if this is what life held for military families, I may as well just get off the planet at the next exit.

And sure enough, helping me towards their same idyllic lifestyle, my cousin Lieutenant Commander Carter the following day introduced me to the Admiral's daughter at a dinner, in his mansion on base. I had never liked to eat lobster, but when in Rome as they say... What's more, I didn't know *how* to eat it properly.

My new friend Anna, the Admiral's daughter would delight in instructing me. I pretended to enjoy the food and his daughter but throughout the evening I was thinking about how Adonis and I would sit next to each other in the mess hall, after a good work-out in the gym.

She also delighted in telling me that her father was being reassigned to Jacksonville, Florida and that they would have a cottage on the beach, having known about my love of cottages and water – but *not* my love of men!

What's more, she knew that my ship would be assigned to Mayport, a stone's throw from Jacksonville and suggested, after I had accidently flung two fully grown lobsters on the dining room floor, that we could see more of each other – maybe even teach me how to crack a prawn's paw.

Rhode Island behind, I headed north to Maine hoping I'd make new friends, while calculating how many nails it would take to keep my closet door firmly shut!

"The once perfectly straight formation of ships was now bugging out left and right in order to get as far away from us as possible."

CHAPTER FOUR:
HERE WE GO!

Hey, people, I joined the Navy to see the world, not to experience bloody freezing New England! Nonetheless, I was *sooo* excited to get to my first ship, the USS *Clifton Sprague* (FFG-16) that I was willing to brave even the coldest state in the Northeast. I relished the idea of going to sea and seeing the big, wide world and all it had to offer!

But *wait*! Not so fast, buckaroo; after only one week in Maine I received TDY (Temporary Duty) orders to NSCS Navy Supply Corps School in Athens, Georgia for six months.

I was glad to be getting out of the frozen north, but it would mean six more months of one of my least favorite aspects of the Navy: *s-c-h-o-o-l*. At least it would be *warmer* there, but... Athens, Georgia? Isn't that inland? There was a navy base, inland? What, did the Navy think the enemy wouldn't know there's a navy base 250 miles inland from the nearest water? Fooled me, too...

What's more, I argued with myself, I hadn't even been to sea yet, and I was getting sea sick from all the different orders and duty stations. How was I supposed to make any long lasting friends with this transient life style?

The Supply Corps was one of the oldest staff corps in the U.S. Navy. I would be trained in supply, logistics, combat support, readiness, contracting and fiscal issues. The official motto of the Supply Corps was "Ready for Sea" – reflecting the Supply Corps' longstanding role in sustaining war fighting. Hello, thank you; I'd been *trying to get to sea* but the military kept *sending to me school ashore!*

School: blah, blah, blah! I don't have to describe it: blackboards, books, and tons of information. Enough already. Let's talk about the men! All of us at Supply Corps School were young, fresh, and eager. On the first day of class, I made one good friend, Ensign Shawn Baker.

He was sitting next to me in the front row. Most of the other Ensigns had made it to the safer back row seats first but, yea you guessed it; me choosing my candy, and my boy slow off the mark – *déjà vu, non?*

The Master Chief entered the classroom looking for any insubordination that could be punished. Still, Ensign Baker leaned towards me bravely and said "Dude, Shawn." I liked him immediately for his bravery—and of course he was the best-looking guy in the class.

For the entire six months in Athens, we worked out at the gym side by side, went out to eat together, and saw movies as often as we could get off base…I'm sure he didn't know, but now I wonder if even I knew we were in effect dating?

His smile was infectious, and we'd often be walking on base, side-by-side – smiling. Officers passing by would glance at us wondering what we knew that they didn't. We both joined the base choir, where I became the Choirmaster, a task I enjoyed; Shawn stood directly in front of me, his big, brown eyes fixed on me while he totally murdered *Anchor's Away*.

Midway through training to earn our Surface Warfare Supply Corps Officer (SWSCO) pin for supply officers serving onboard a ship we all got a week of leave. Since we'd been spending so much time together, it seemed natural when Shawn suggested we take a day-trip to Lookout Mountain in Tennessee.

Being the bravest of the couple, it was his idea to take a hang-gliding lesson; I wished I could have been equally brave and actually said something about how I was feeling, but I knew that was impossible. The consequences, both in our friendship and in the Navy, would have been disastrous.

Oh, but if only we could have just flown away together, and land somewhere where we could be together forever! I let myself dream as we soared in the air next to each other.

However, we missed the designated landing field, and came down in a cow pasture, littered with land mines of hardened cow dung that exploded their moist contents all over us upon impact, a perfect come-down to my crazy fantasies

On the way back to Athens, I asked Shawn if we could stop in Chattanooga, Tennessee so I could see the famed Chattanooga Choo-Choo train. I loved ships and trains, and always liked to see one, although many of them in their declining years just get parked, and turned into hotels.

He was indifferent, yet obliging about seeing the train until he learned it was now a hotel. With sudden enthusiasm he suggested we stay the night. With my heart pounding, and my skin covered with nervous sweat, I cautioned him that the Master Chief would probably send the National Guard, with blood-hounds and helicopters, to look for us if we were even a second late returning to base.

What would have happened if he'd convinced me we should stay overnight? Or even the remainder of our week-long leave off-base together. I'm still not sure, and still wonder if he would have wanted the time to pass the same way I did.

My fantasies galloped ahead of me as we road back to the base. If I'd had to share a bed with him, or even a room, there would certainly have been embarrassing moments—moments I wasn't ready to risk. No matter how much I wanted to share a room, a bed, a life with the guy, I couldn't risk it, and so we returned to the base, safe, but sorry.

Back at school, few of us had a car for the six-month assignment. What's more, since Athens was small geographically with moderate weather, mountain bikes gave us ease of mobility. Shawn was simple and down to earth (just how I liked them), but a real head turner everywhere we went together on our bikes because of his incredible good looks.

One night, I tried to upgrade his life experiences by taking him to a French restaurant in a converted old Victorian mansion downtown, where the staff gave us unmistakable looks: they themselves were obviously gay, and assumed we were, too. "Back off guys," I said with just a glance when we first walked in, "I saw him first."

Perhaps I was also testing him, to see how he'd respond to this obviously gay-friendly venue, which would have provided me a definitive answer as to why he had wanted to get a hotel room together. But the dinner revealed nothing about his proclivities, and only showed that he didn't know the difference between moules frites and mélange de fruits.

Weeks later, sitting next to him in the once- again stultifying classroom, I looked over at him wistfully. I felt like I was losing him, so I resolved to switch our dining venue on our next date to Athens' most popular fried catfish "restaurant" ...if you can call it that.

It was in the mosquito-infested woods, about as far from civilization as Athens was from the sea. As for the clientele? Well, let's say it gave me a reference point from which to evaluate everyone else on the planet I was soon to meet as my horizons would expand beyond Georgia.

And not soon enough I thought, sitting on the toilet giving them back their catfish, while reading on the stall wall "I try to figure out my family tree, but now say why bother, for my father got married one more time, now my sister is my mother." This bit of local poetry was even signed by its eloquent author, C Drane!

"Oh yeah?" I challenged the author, in my final few seconds in that literary den. Fumbling for a pen in my jeans that were around my ankles, I began my own composition on the wall "My mother spit me out on the back seat of a Harley, while telling the State Trooper to go screw himself, all without the cigarette even falling from her lips!" It was neither rhyming, nor perhaps the correct local syntax, but at least I was trying to fit in! Flush...

Returning from the toilet, I realized that Shawn was much more at ease here. Yet, even though I had finally found what my man liked, school was nearly over and we would be moving on to our permanent duty assignments.

I still think of him often: his broad, honest smile with a slight tilt of his head, and of course how he looked in a crisp white tank top over tight jean shorts, especially after we had ridden our bikes for hours and a sweat blended our thin shirts into our muscled chests. I honestly think he knew I *looked* at him, and it didn't bother him – he'd just *look* right back at me and smile while flexing his chest muscles for me to enjoy.

I also decided he simply didn't like French food, and overtly gay men. Perhaps our friendship could have developed into a relationship had I not been afraid of being discharged and losing my commission so soon. The inevitability of military orders tore us apart and saved me from having to choose him, or the military.

My consolation in parting from Shawn was that I was now heading to Maine and to my first ship. And it wasn't even finished yet. What an odd place to build huge weapons of mass destruction: a small, quaint village in Maine. Were we trying to fool anyone, fellows? The ship's mast was taller than the church steeple; I *think* it was obvious what was going on here.

Once completed and launched, our ship put out to sea quietly, with neither pomp nor circumstance. Hey, I could have at least broken a bottle of beer on the bow...well, *if* I drank beer. How about a bottle of Chateau Lafayette Reneau?

Never mind, could we just finally *go to sea*?

OK, I was going to kill myself because apparently, when navy ships get underway, it's not so quietly after all. Once the anchor is secured, or moorings freed they each play their chosen trademark "getting underway" music – usually starting as they passed the outer buoy.

So, imagine a fisherman in his dinghy early one frosty morning, being passed by our enormous battleship-grey weapon of mass destruction that was blaring out over the 1mc "On the Road Again" by Willie Nelson! Engineman Bowman had suggested it to the skipper, and since they were both from the South, it was a unanimous two vote decision.

Once at sea, we would join our task force for training exercises and sea trials. I had learned that our sister ship, the USS *Sampson* (DDG10), played "Ride of the Valkyries" from the German "Walkurenritt," the beginning of Act III of *Die Walkure* by Richard Wagner. Now, that was more to my liking. If you're going out to sea, shouldn't it be to the strains of something classic, grand and majestic, not a worn-out country song?

What's more, the *Sampson* was a classic herself. She had also been built in Bath some years before the *Sprague*, and was a Charles F Adams class diesel destroyer, which meant her profile was long, low and graceful – ours was top-heavy and clumsy.

As ungraciously as my military service would one day end so to would hers in 1991 when she would be decommissioned, and in 1992 when she would be sold for scrap!

But before that would occur, we both were serving our country honorably. Leaving the *Sprague's* bridge wing behind, the sounds of trumpets from the *Sampson* fading, I blurted towards our bridge, "Can I be transferred to the *Sampson*? No, really, I mean it."

To which our skipper replied without budging from the comfort of his bridge chair, "Get the hell off my bridge!"

Walking dejectedly back to the bridge wing, my mood changed and I was filled with pride when I saw six ships in a long straight formation, just like the movies from World War II. God, I loved this job. We were about to conduct live missile tests, which meant real, armed missiles being fired at a real target.

At this point in my career, I was just the Supply Officer and so not part of the drill, although technically I ordered the missiles and technically I ensured they got onboard. Nonetheless, I was allowed on the bridge to observe. "Missile is away," reported the Fire Control Officer, followed by a swish, then a boom sound. All ships fired in turn with the same resulting swish, then boom.

"Hey, this has been fun watching you boys with your toys, but I'm hungry and I'm going to the galley," I sighed.

As I slid down the ladder from the bridge, I thought I heard a ditty: "There once was a sailor from Lee, that was plumbing a girl by the sea, said the girl 'Stop your plumbing, there is someone coming' now said the sailor still plumbing, 'Jiz me.'"

Once below, while looking for my forty-five caliber pistol in order to stop the ditty from replaying itself in my head, I heard the repeated swish...boom, swish...boom as I gnawed on a cold sandwich in the galley (the galley fires are out during drills). Then, just a swish was heard from our ship's launcher—no boom. "What?" I thought, pausing with mouth full and turning an ear aloft.

Running aft, sandwich still in hand, I poked my head though the small four foot square escape hatch in the flight deck above my office and felt my heart in my throat as I saw our live missile in the air coming right towards us, and flying directly over our flight deck inches from my head! Then it dove into the water and I quickly realized that the approaching water plume was our own live missile, now seeking us as its target! Hey, I only ordered the damn thing from the Supply Depot; I didn't hit "fire."

The once-perfectly straight formation of ships was now bugging out left and right in order to get as far away from us, and the imminent explosion, as possible. Only the mighty USS New Jersey (BB62) directly astern would stay with us. She was now slowing, turning sluggishly to port, while her three massive gun turrets were maneuvering to starboard towards us.

Great, I'd been at sea for one week and I was about to be killed by friendly fire, I shivered while bracing for ...

The New Jersey fired a broadside: nine, twenty-seven hundred pound, sixteen inch long shells each propelled by eight, forty-five pound bags of gunpowder in a fifty foot tall cloud of smoke and fire. Needless to say, our rogue missile was destroyed, and just yards before it killed us. Even though she hadn't been fully reactivated yet, the grande dame had returned from moth balls in time to save the new kids on the block.

Crewmen in our laundry would later reveal to me that our Officer of the Deck had literally wet his pants.

The Supply Officer on the New Jersey was probably picking up his sandwich because when his battleship had fired the broadside that had destroyed our rogue missile, all of New Jersey's forty five thousand tons had moved six feet in the opposite direction of the shoot, and from where he had probably been standing in the mess deck.

It would take us a couple of days to steam back to port and determine why we had just tried to blow ourselves up. As Morale Officer, it was up to me to decide when to show a movie, so in order to calm everyone down; I decided to have a movie shown that night on the mess deck. But at 20:00 hours—showtime–I was still leaning through the window of the store towards the clerk, waiting for the cash drawer and daily receipts so I could put them in the safe. "Would you hurry up, sailor, the movie is about to start!"

"Yes, Sir" Petty Officer Ashford replied formally, while fumbling with the drawer and dropping its contents onto the deck. He too was obviously shaken by the day's events. With my head still in the store window, and my butt in the passage way, I felt someone rub against me from behind and say "Do you want this, Ensign?"

It was cute Thomas Bowman from the South, perhaps the author of the ditty I had heard earlier that day. He had a pleasant, slow drawl and a chaw in his mouth at all times. I withdrew from the ship's store window, turned around slowly, looked directly into his eyes, and called his bluff by saying with authority, "Sure, my place or yours, Engineman Bowman?"

Military discipline had been maintained, so he spit into his paper cup, smiled, and sauntered towards where we could hear the movie had already started.

A short time later, I sat at the rear of the mess deck next to one of my Ship Servicemen, a nice young Filipino boy who worked in the laundry. In the darkness of the mess deck punctuated only by the flickering light on the movie screen, he leaned towards me and whispered, "Thanks, Mr. B." I smiled back at him in the darkness, and gently poked his ribs with my elbow. I wasn't sure what he was thanking me for, the movie... for sitting next to him...or just my being one of the officers on the ship that actually cared about the crew.

I leaned back and sighed. If that sigh could have been translated, it would have spoken volumes about what I was feeling but didn't dare speak aloud. I would have loved to lean over, put my arm around his slim shoulders, and comfort him to the point of distraction.

And I couldn't. We shared closeness—the closeness of having survived a truly terrifying event—and yet I couldn't express the closeness I felt for him. Or the attraction I felt for some of the other men.

Instead, I had to sit there, palms firmly on my own knees or arms crossed over my chest, watching *For Your Eyes Only* again.

The next morning during my routine bunk inspection, I would find this same Ship Serviceman in his rack crying. I sat next to him, placed my hand gently on his shoulder and asked what was wrong. He got up slowly, without removing my hand and said "Mr. B, my wife is pregnant, due any day and I want to be with her." I smiled to myself.

I liked it that my men called me "Mr. B." Or they would stand at attention on deck, in linear formation at the crack of dawn for morning quarters, and wait until I was within earshot for one among them to shriek "Oh no, Mr. Bill." I would pretend not to hear.

However, one of my crewmembers in distress was no laughing matter, and I knew I had to do something to help him out. After I pleaded his case with the skipper, he was given a brief three days shore leave to be with his wife, which would commence the moment we got back in port at Bath.

The sea spray on my face was exhilarating as I stood at the bow of the ship, her sharp nose slicing though the Atlantic Sea (her nose, which houses the sonar dome, actually looks like Jimmy Durante's). Then, leaning over the deck railing and glancing towards the stern of the ship, I saw the white caps in our wake created by this powerful machine that would take me – back to Bath, Maine! "Hey, deep-water is *that direction*," I shouted towards the bridge while motioning pleadingly in the opposite direction, towards where I wanted to go. "How am I going to get my diving certification if you head back to shallow water?" I sighed disappointingly.

Since we had just nearly sunk this new toy, we now had to be good little boys and go back to our room until we were told we could come out again, while the Navy tried to figure out what had gone wrong and how to keep it from happening again.

Meantime, I'd be a good little boy and continue quashing my feelings—or some of them, anyway—for my fellow men.

I'd learned that I could show some of my feelings, like by using my position as Morale Officer to help get their minds off our near-miss with a live missile by showing a movie, or by helping a young crewman get a three-day leave to see his wife and their newborn.

Maybe, since I loved my work so much, this would be enough.

Maybe, at least for now.

"The ship was in a trough... rolling violently. 'One of is going to wear dinner.'"

Don't Ask, Do Tell

CHAPTER FIVE:
On the Road Again

Weeks later from the galley I heard "On the Road Again" and got chicken skin as I stumbled towards the bridge. We were finally going out to sea again!

I materialized on the bridge with my diving gear, like a boy at the beach with his snorkel and fins on the first day of summer.

Steaming south towards the deep water of the vast Atlantic Ocean, I smiled and couldn't help but shout out loud, "God, I love this job. When do we eat?"

Apparently that was up to me as I was the Supply Officer in charge of the mess hall for the enlisted men and the wardroom for the officers.

Now, the mess hall stewards were chosen by my subordinate the MSC (Chief of the Mess), and the job was used as a form of punishment: screw up as a deckhand (where you got to be on deck all day, looking at the ocean) and you would get sent to the bowels of the ship to sweat in the mess. And I thought the men on the *Nina*, the *Pinta*, and the *Santa Maria* had it rough?

The wardroom was staffed by *moi*, so since I was in charge, I cherry-picked who I wanted from the deck crew; smooth-skin, pretty eyes, modest size (*never* overweight), and the ability to take orders—was this heaven?

Years later I would become good friends with Lieutenant Commander George Evans, who had held the same position on his ship, and who had exactly the same selection process for wardroom stewards for exactly the same reasons (insert nod and wink here). So it must have been some sort of Navy tradition, yeah? I doubted I would ever have to defend my selection process at a Board of Inquiry.

Another tradition was that when in rough seas, before each meal you thoroughly soaked the tablecloth with water, wrung it out—leaving it damp—and placed it back on the table in the wardroom. Subsequently, the china wouldn't slide off the table. Well, in theory.

One night, during especially stormy seas, my beauties were serving the officers in the wardroom, watching me and taking cues from me like good little soldiers as the officers put their heads to their plates and shoveled away; one sideways nod meant "remove the service," one forward nod told my wait staff "bring the next course." It was simple, but effective.

The pace of the meal was set by the captain, who I watched from directly across the table as diligently as my staff was watching me: If he ate as fast as a farm animal, I ensured that so did we all and that the service kept pace with my signals to the staff.

However, no one had been trained to interpret what rapid left to right movement of my head signaled. But on this night, with the waves raising and pitching the ship like it was a cork, it was obvious to all in the wardroom that someone was about to wear dinner!

The long wardroom table ran port to starboard. On this night, the ship was in a trough, which meant she was rolling violently and continuously from port to starboard. The captain was at one end of the table and I was at my strategic vantage point opposite him.

With one huge swell, the table tilted toward me, and I saw the plates sliding in my direction despite the wetted tablecloth. A hesitation, and then it reversed, tilting toward him. As the ship pitched and rolled, we looked each other in the eye with a challenge. Our eyes seem to say to each other, "You're going to wear the spaghetti with marinara sauce, not me."

"Red suits you," I surmised a few seconds later, after I had won the battle. He looked squarely at me, let out a belly laugh, and said, "God, I love this job." Hey, that was *my* line!

In the crew's mess, there was no tablecloth, and no china. During rough seas, a steel lip could be raised round the edge of the tables, preventing the dinner trays from sliding onto the deck.

That was a week in which not only the weather was rough.

Early the next morning as I was making my rounds, I went into the wardroom for a coffee and to see how the breakfast service was coming along. Long faces on all my beauties. "What's the matter?" I asked the four of them who were standing around looking forlorn as they cracked eggs into a giant bowl.

They looked at each other sheepishly. "Well?" I persisted gently. And then Seaman Recruit Jack Hayden told me; after dinner the previous night, two crewmembers had been caught "doing it" in the helicopter hangar, and had been summarily flown off the ship during the night.

My heart sank, and a jolt of fear went through me.

If they were caught, would that mean that eyes would be watching to see if there were others who were possibly gay, like, for example, *moi?* Even though I was staying with my promise not to engage in any activities that could get me booted, this was enough to put me on my guard.

But I was also shocked. How was it possible that others were "doing it" secretly and I was suffering alone? This was the first time I really considered that others were connecting, while I wasn't, and this made me question my stance—but not enough to change what I was doing (or wasn't doing).

Turning back towards the tiny galley, and my four favorites I said softly "You boys just be careful, *non*?" I guessed they were playing on the same team, but I didn't know how much they were acting on their inclinations.

Now, had I known for a fact that these four, and others on the ship, were gay and not reported it; I too would have been removed from the ship. However, to date all I had had was my gut instinct about them.

Years later, one of those four, Jack, would find me in the Gay.com chat room. He filled in all the blanks, and confirmed I was correct in many regards as to what gay activity was taking place on the ship. I was happy to learn that after he left active duty, Jack had met a man with whom he was still in a ten year, loving relationship!

After the bust of the two crewmembers, tension on the ship was palpable: the careers of two young men had ended. But the duty of those of us remaining onboard continued unabated.

Even as their names were being muttered in hushed tones throughout the ship, we suddenly heard "General quarters, general quarters – all hands man you battle stations..." blare out over the 1mc interspersed with gong, gong, gong from the ships alarm system.

Personal conversations ceased, hatches were secured, and helmeted crewmembers reported, with hearts beating rapidly, manned and ready from their pre-assigned battle stations – in less than sixty seconds. In equally short order we learned it had been just a drill.

Way to go, skipper, that would keep everyone focused! He could have given me at least a ten minute warning, time enough to get my soufflé out of the oven before reporting to my GQ station in the Helicopter Control Tower!

As our journey south continued, I participated in yet another Navy tradition: the reenlistment ceremony. When a crewmember decided that he, too, loved this job and wanted to "reup" for four more years, he reenlisted by taking an oath given by an officer of his choice.

"Me, they really want *me*?" I said humbly to the captain, while noting out of the corner of my eye the jealousy of all the other officers.

We always made as much fun as we could out of these ceremonies—hey; there wasn't a whole lot to do for entertainment when you were a six-day, six-week, or maybe even a six-month journey from any shore.

So there I was on the enlisted mess deck once again. The ensemble included a handsome officer wearing his dress blue uniform (yours truly), a young man with a white beard (playing Father Time), and my cute Filipino boy, now back onboard a new father and himself in a diaper (playing Baby New Year). The theme and costumes of reenlistments was by crewmember choice—hey; I didn't make these rules and traditions!

Repeat after me; "I, Father Time and Baby new Year, in lieu of going to prison, swear to sign away four years of my life to the United States Navy because I want to hang out with Marines without actually having to *be* one of them, because I thought the Air Force was too corporate, and because I thought, hey, I like to swim...why not?" I began the oath, looking up with a start from the page I had been reciting from, and towards smiling faces. Shaking my head disapprovingly at their chosen words I continued:

"I promise to wear clothing that went out of style in 1976 and to have my name stenciled on the butt of every pair of pants I own. I understand that I will be mistaken for the Good Humor man during the summer and for Waffen SS during the winter." I paused to clear my throat, and steal a laugh of my own before looking back down at the paper and continued to read:

"I will strive to use a different language than the rest of the English-speaking world, using words like deck, bulkhead, cover, and head instead of floor, wall, hat, and toilet. I will take great pride in the fact that all Navy acronyms rank and insignias, and everything else for that matter, are completely different from the other services and make absolutely no sense whatsoever."

"I will muster at 0700 hours every morning unless I am buddy-buddy with the Chief, in which case I will show up around 0930 hours."

"I vow to hone my coffee cup handling skills to the point that I can stand up in a kayak being tossed around in a typhoon, and still not spill a drop."

"I consent to being promoted and subsequently busted at least twice per fiscal year. I realize that, once selected for Chief, I am required to submit myself to the sick, and quite possibly illegal, whims of my new-found colleagues."

The oath given, Father Time shook my hand, and Baby New Year jumped into my arms and kissed me. A howl ensued, replete with guffaws, but hey—it was all good fun, yeah?

Nonetheless, in order to divert attention from the kiss that I had enjoyed, I recited from C Drane "People say we can't be in love, but I think they're full of bleep, because I am a strapping young man, and you're a cute-assed sheep."

The mess deck was the setting for many of our most memorable events. Some months after the re-up ceremony, at 0430 hours I rousted my crew from sleep and had them assemble without explanation.

Their reaction was less than loving, I surmised from their sleepy faces and their cautiously muffled expletives.

From almost day one on that ship, I had secretly been writing to the family members of each of my men. Knowing that we would be at sea over Christmas, I had solicited gifts for them from their respective families, with the provision it be kept a secret—until Christmas morning.

"I know its zero dark thirty, and I know we are in the middle of bloody nowhere on Christmas day, in this tin can that is now our home" I spoke with mock authority. "I just wanted to be the first to wish you all a merry Christmas" I finished with a smile, while removing a borrowed parachute that had been covering all their gifts.

The young Filipino Ship Serviceman emerged from the chaos of present-opening and handed me a sheet of paper. "What's this?" I asked him softly.

"I had the first watch last night, Christmas Eve, and wrote this for you, Mr. B, because of what you did for us," he replied, looking at me for my reaction.

"But, how did you know?" I shot back. "No one was supposed to know until Christmas morning," I continued with mock anger.

"Ensign, did you *honestly* think we wouldn't notice all those boxes you tried to hide in the boatswain's locker?" he said with a twisted smile.

With a laugh in response, while glancing at the chaos, I then looked down at the paper he had handed me and read:

'Twas the night before Christmas,

The ship was out steaming,

Sailors stood watch while others were dreaming.

We lived in a crowd with racks tight and small,

In an 80-man berthing, cramped one and all.

I looked all about, a strange sight did I see,

No tinsel, no presents, not even a tree.

No stockings were hung, shined boots close at hand,

On the bulkhead hung pictures, of a far distant land.

We had medals and badges and awards of all kind,

And sober thoughts came into my mind.

For now it was different, as some had come back,

While others had not, nor lie in their rack.

As I lay sleeping, silent and alone,

I curl up in my sack and dream of home.

My face is gentle, the room squared away,

I know that tomorrow will bring, a fun filled day.

I realized Ensign Bonzo would visit this night,

Bringing joy to these sailors who lay willing to fight.

Soon round the ship, all would play,

As Mr. B would announce "Voila, it's Christmas Day."

Americans enjoy freedom each day of the year,

Because of sailors, like the one lying here.

I couldn't help wonder how many lay alone,

On this cold Christmas Eve at sea, far from home.

The very thought brought a tear to my eye,

I tried to sleep, but started to cry.

Then I heard the Ensign's calm voice,

"Hey, don't cry, this life is our choice."

"Defending the seas all days of the year,

So others may live and be free with no fear."

I thought for a moment, what a difficult road,

To live a life guided by honor and code.

After all it's Christmas Eve and the ship is underway,

But freedom isn't free and it's sailors who pay.

The sailor says to our country "be free and sleep tight,

No harm will come, not on my watch and not on this night."

I rolled over, and drifted to sleep,

But couldn't control it, and continued to weep.

Mr. B had the watch, so silent, so still,

He stood on the bridge, and shivered from the night's cold chill.

Looking dapper in his bridge coat, on that cold dark night,

He was a guardian of honor, so willing to fight.

The ship's bell rang midnight, and with a voice strong and sure,

He commanded, "Carry on, it's Christmas, and all is Secure!"

Looking up from the poem I had been reading, and directly into the author's eyes I winked and said "Do you really think that bridge coat looks good on me?"

And so our journey on the ship continued, with the memory of the two men who'd we lost to the Navy's policies fading in the routine that is shipboard life.

But they were not forgotten by me, or by many others who perhaps were now more cautious and more afraid.

"Just feed me the damned shaving cream pie and be done with it!"

Don't Ask, Do Tell

CHAPTER SIX:
RITE OF PASSAGE

There was one Navy tradition, which had I known about in advance I would have changed the ship's course, opened a hatch and taken on water, or just plain jumped overboard (which I had been trained to do, remember?)—the rite of passage suffered when crossing the equator.

This imaginary line on the earth's surface is equidistant from the North and South Poles, and divides the earth into the Northern Hemisphere and the Southern Hemisphere. So what could the big deal be about crossing it?

The tradition began with French ships in the 16th century. At first the pagan rites were performed when ships passed around a major cape safely for the first time, but as time went on, this hazing celebration was extended to all sailors who passed the equator for the first time.

The original equator-crossing ceremony was a serious event, and a rite of passage for each sailor who had never before crossed the equator – they called it going from being a "pollywog" to being called a "shellback."

And even though paganism would give way to Christianity, sailors of old remained a superstitious bunch, and would do anything to appease the treacherous seas.

The English eventually followed the practice in the next century, with even Captain James Cook writing about it in his journals. In Cook's day, the ship heaved to and the Pollywogs were hoisted over the seas by the mainyard and were dunked into the ocean water 30-40 feet below them. If the Pollywog was an officer of the ship, whose dignity wouldn't allow such a dunking, he had to forfeit pay, usually in the way of bottles of rum for the after-dunking party.

Even Franklin D. Roosevelt was put through this same rite of passage. From the Department of the Navy Historical Center, here are some of the excerpts from the subpoena served to him:

To Franklin D. Roosevelt: You will accept heartily and with good grace the pains and penalties of the awful torture that will be inflicted upon you to determine your fitness to be one of our trusty Shellbacks and answer to the following charges:

Charge 1: Disregard of the traditions of the sea, having failed to appear in person to show allegiance to his Royal Highness, thereby masquerading as a man of the sea, and by this utter disregard added insult to other crimes.

Charge 2: Taking liberties with the piscatorial subjects of His Majesty Neptunus Rex, and having taken liberties with the denizens of the Realm of Neptunus Rex, by maliciously removing them from the depths of their recognized habitat and has exaggerating this crime by public humiliation of the greatest of these creatures of the sea by stuffing them full of sawdust, and placing them in a position of eternal disgrace in a national museum where the eyes of all mortals may disregard their pitiful and ignoble plight.

Neptunus Rex

Ruler of the Raging Main

"Captain Cook was killed by the Hawaiians, so the tradition died with him, *non*?" I would plead unsuccessfully, to the delight of my crew, while I was being led, hands bound, to the flight deck... Today, we were re-enacting the ceremony for fun, and to relieve shipboard monotony so for *the crew's* sake, I complied.

"Eager to please the ancient god of the sea, Neptune, the humiliation you will suffer, and fines you will pay are a small price to get Neptune's blessing," I heard as I reached the flight deck, and was made prone and given the opportunity to plead my case against the imminent hazing.

"You have been hereby commanded to appear before the Royal Court of the Realm of Neptune, in the District of Equatorius, because it has been brought to the attention of His Highness, Neptune Rex, through his trusty Shellbacks, that this ship about to enter those waters is manned by some crewmembers who have not acknowledged the sovereignty of the Ruler Of The Deep, and has transgressed on his domain and thereby incurred his Royal displeasure," I heard from the Master Chief, aka Davy Jones, standing above me.

"Do you have anything to say in your defense, Ensign Bonzo?" he continued in an affected voice that I desperately tried *not* to laugh at on this auspicious occasion.

"Enough already with the ear-piercing *horrific* use of the English language," I begged King Neptune upon hearing the same charges as President Roosevelt had heard, "Just feed me the damned shaving cream pie, and be done with it!"

Neptune now appeared before all us Pollywogs groveling on the deck and put us through a sort of college fraternity-like hazing, which demanded us to eat globs of grossly concocted food combinations that the cook had made up, possibly including my now moldy, failed soufflé. The fun also included dousing with buckets of salt water, among other humiliating feats, all in the presence of the Shellbacks on board.

I worked mightily to remember that I had *volunteered* to join the Navy.

One more military tradition was completed, and there were how many more to go? As I had a long shower after achieving my own

Shellback status, I calculated that there were hundreds of years of seafaring experience, and all affixed to a swelling number of naval traditions!

I knew that Churchill was credited with saying that the three traditions of the British Navy were "rum, sodomy and the lash." Maybe not all naval traditions were such a bad thing, after all?

Back in uniform, I entered the Wardroom for a cup of tea. "Are you alright, son?" said the Captain paternally.

"Sure, Skipper," I replied with mock enthusiasm, "I just love being abused by grown men while in a prone position." The cute Wardroom steward on duty, Seaman Recruit Jack Hayden, smiled knowingly at the metaphor and me as he brought me my tea.

Before the skipper could put one and one together to get the sum of the understanding relationship between Jack and me, I engaged him in a distracting, and completely off-the-subject conversation. "How did the British get the nick-name Pommie?" I solicited from his years of experience.

"It stands for Prisoner of Mother England," he said. "An acronym of 'Prisoner of His Majesty', which was stamped on the uniforms of prisoners transferred to Botany Bay in Australia. However, many historians dispute this claim," he finished abruptly as if doubting his own words.

Glancing quickly towards the steward, I caught him rolling his eyes, smiled at him, and returned my gaze to the skipper for further enlightenment. "So, what then is a Tommy?" I asked with affected sincerity.

"The name Tommy was for any soldier in the British Army, and was particularly associated with World War I," he supplied the information readily. "It derived from the name Tommy Atkins," he continued without hesitation, "In a poem published by Rudyard Kipling (*the Barrack Room Ballads*) published in 1892."

Jack and I were standing motionless, each bug-eyed, and speechless that the Skipper had taken my bait. We were also both curious where he was going with it.

Now it was the skipper's turn to smile at us both, as he added from the experience of his years, during our paralysis "Now, during those decades, 'nanshoku' became used to refer to..." and he stopped his dialogue short, looking first squarely at me, then at Seaman Recruit Hayden.

Pulling from my general knowledge of just about everything, I knew that nanshoku, as well as shudo and wakashudo, were words used to refer to homosexual behavior during the late Edo period in Japan. I also realized frightfully, that perhaps I wasn't doing such a good job of hiding the fact that I was gay – or was he just fishing?

"I would much rather have been at sea, going somewhere..."

CHAPTER SEVEN:
MAYPORT, FLORIDA

One should never have too much of a good thing, so eventually we entered port at Mayport, Florida, our home base.

Now, I would much rather have been at sea, going somewhere, even if it included degrading public rituals. However, so long as the boat was firmly tied to the pier and wasn't going anywhere, I figured I may as well stretch my legs.

And we were going to have a nice, long stretch—we'd be there for at least two years, I was led to believe by my superiors.

I rented a house with another new Ensign whose ship was also recently assigned to Mayport. I was big and muscled and Ensign Fisher was lean and fit. We were the perfect couple except for one thing: his girlfriend!

When we had signed the lease, subject to military orders as were most leases to military personnel, I was excited to finally have a house, with another man. I had envisioned cooking for him, the two of us lying on the sofa watching TV together, brushing my teeth while he took a shower and we discussed the duty assignments for the day, and so forth. And while all of this came to pass, his girlfriend was a constant reminder to me that he was lucky enough to have a relationship I craved, and I was not.

It was only a short walk from the house to the base entrance gate, as the crow flies, but after just a few weeks I decided one day to just take my time, and took the long route through the sand dunes along the water. I passed the adorable, small cottages that dotted Jacksonville Beach, knowing that most of them belonged to higher-ranking military officers including the Admiral, Anna's father.

What the hell was I thinking? Did I really think it would ever go anywhere living in that house with a fellow officer? One thing I was certain of was that the situation was frustrating and made me feel even lonlier.

I quickly moved back into my stateroom on board the ship. The rental of the house would have been expensive monetarily and emotionally, and I'd been packing away my pay while at sea. So with the money I saved from the house, and the savings I'd been stockpiling, I bought my first car: a brand new Mercedes.

Nothing smells, feels, sounds, or drives like a new Mercedes. Her diesel engine made her slow off the mark, as was Adonis from boot camp, but they were both also real lookers!

Soon, my new one-and-a-half ton best friend and I were taking mini-vacations together.

One weekend we headed up to historically-beautiful, laid-back Savannah, Georgia. Another trip was over to non-stop sensory overload in Orlando, Florida. The farther from Mayport my Mercedes and I got, the better I felt. I wasn't looking for a man on these brief trips; there wouldn't have been enough time to get to know one even if I had met one, and I wasn't the sort who would want an anonymous quickie.

I loved my life at sea, but my car gave me what the ship couldn't: freedom—freedom to go to a luxury hotel with a deep soaking tub where I could immerse myself in a *Playgirl* magazine that I had purchased, trying to conceal it at the store counter between *Time* and *Newsweek*. It certainly didn't satisfy my emotional longings, but provided a degree of sexual satisfaction, and allowed me to just be who I really was, even if alone and briefly.

The following morning, I would always have a full breakfast, wondering why no one in America knew how to poach an egg, and why grits eaten in the south have butter and salt, while grits in the north are taken with milk and sugar. My German friend was equally finicky; taking only diesel fuel and 30W-50 oil, once we were both sated we'd head back to Mayport and my closeted life onboard the ship.

Over the months, these mini-getaways multiplied, as did my frustration at not having someone special in my life to take on my trips:

from Mayport to Key West, Mayport to Tampa, Mayport to St. Augustine. The trips weren't exactly escapist, because they gave me plenty of time to think about what I was running from, and where I was going.

Given the oppressive nature of life for gay men and lesbians, I started thinking that I had as much chance of finding a relationship while in the military as Christopher Columbus had had of finding India in the Caribbean.

On my trip to the heart-breakingly quaint coastal town of St. Augustine, I found an outdoor concert on the town green, wandered over, and found myself a spot on the lawn. The band was playing Tchaikovsky's *1812 Overture*. I sat there, listening to the music, my thoughts ranging from the sea to my decision to re-up to my disappointment about my failed attempt at keeping house with Ensign Fisher. There was a slight breeze, cooling the warm summer air. Here I was, in a perfect, romantic setting, knowing that I couldn't share it with someone.

At the end of the concert, the cannon fire and cymbals crashing woke me from my reverie, and a chill went through me, even though I had no way of knowing that soon I'd be hearing the real thing in battle.

"Fluency in French helped explain my 'refined' ways on this cruise."

Don't Ask, Do Tell

CHAPTER EIGHT: WHICH WAY IS THE BEACH?

We departed Mayport, Florida for a destination somewhere in the Caribbean. I thought all those Top Secret messages I was required to read every morning were dull, so I paid less attention to them than to what was for breakfast, and therefore didn't know exactly where we were headed. We were at sea, and that's what mattered to me.

As he navigated the ship toward Martinique, the skipper remembered that there was someone on board who could communicate with the French-speaking natives—*moi*—and quickly I was pressed into service as translator.

"Get Bonzo up here, and have him tell these damned Frogs that we need food, fuel, and ship-to-shore service," our eloquent skipper blurted out to the First Officer on the bridge.

Fluency in French gave me some importance on this cruise and, more importantly, helped explain my "refined ways." Bonzo is, after all, a French name; because the final "n" is silent in French, it was lost during my family's immigration to the Americas, resulting in the name change from Bonzon to Bonzo. Thank God the middle "n" was pronounced.

But, just *how* had Ronald Reagan's chimp gotten the name Bonzo, too? In response to my written inquiry to him, his secretary responded politely that I should contact Universal studios for the information. I also received a signed picture of Reagan with the chimp on his knee! Perhaps Ronald was just cleaning out his desk and wanted to finally get rid of the picture.

"Oui, mon Ca-pi-tan," I said as I climbed the ladder of the bridge. One does want a hint of humor, *non*? I caught a brief smile on the skipper's face, only to have the First Officer land a quarter of an inch from my face repeating the command to start making sense of these "Frogs," as the skipper so eloquently put it.

Martinique is an island in the eastern Caribbean Sea. It is an overseas region of France, consisting of a single overseas department. As with the other overseas departments, Martinique is one of the twenty-six regions of France and an integral part of the Republic. At least there was a good chance the food would be good. And indeed it was.

Later that evening on our first day in port, the officers from our ship were to be the guests of honor at a gala dinner hosted by the Conseil Regional Martinique.

"I can't breathe in this thing, let alone swallow any food," I said, tugging at the collar of my dress "choker white" uniform while listening to the familiar sound of *La Marseillaise* in Fort-de-France.

Nonetheless, I did manage to eat, and eat, and eat! "*Vive la France*," I said between mouthfuls, only to be rudely stopped by our skipper, who said, "Play for them, Bonzo."

"Do I look like a monkey who plays for his dinner? I mean, I do realize the name Bonzo, and everything..." I sighed while slamming the silverware onto the table.

Wiping the *foie gras* delicately from each side of my mouth with a crisp linen napkin, I acquiesced. Mounting a beautiful well-legged Pleyel grand piano, I played for my dinner, closing my eyes the better to remember the notes.

When I opened my eyes, having finished *Carnival of Animals* (appropriate, *non*?), by Camille Saint-Saens, I saw there was a woman sitting on the bench next to me! "What—a door prize?" I thought. I learned that she was the daughter of the Conseil, but I didn't sit around long enough to find out if I was being set-up with her, or if the music had simply lured her to my side.

Martinique and its food were disappearing on the horizon behind us as we set course and got underway for the Panama Canal, where my ever-caring and ever-naïve fellow officers were about to help me get laid.

Situated on the isthmus connecting North and South America, Panama is bordered by Costa Rica to the northwest, Colombia to the southeast, the Caribbean Sea to the north, and the Pacific Ocean to the south. The capital is Panama City.

Captain Antonio Tello de Guzman got here before me in 1515, stopping in a small indigenous fishing town by the name of Panama. It's believed that the word "Panama" means "abundance of fish, trees, and butterflies."

Panama is also now an international business center and has the third or fourth largest economy in Central America. An abundant portion of that "business" is the oldest profession in the world, I was about to learn.

On my birthday, a group of the officers told me they wanted to take me out to dinner, so I put on my going-out civvies outfit: a lightweight Le Coq Sportif cotton jacket, a polo shirt, and jeans, thinking my fellow officers were risking arrest by the Panamanian fashion police in their cargo shorts and stained t-shirts.

"Nope, none, not a one of them knows how to dress or act in public," I concluded as we all walked a dimly lit, cobblestone street towards a local bar.

Inside, it was what you'd expect: dimly lit, with a few American servicemen at the bar in a small group. My tip-off was that the only women were strutting around in very tight, very short dresses; it was obvious what their line of work was.

Before I knew it, my officers had set me up with one, proclaiming this was my birthday gift:

"one that would open itself" one of the guys crowed, laughing as if this was the funniest thing ever said.

Less than thirty minutes after entering the bar, I was leaving, accompanied by the woman they'd chosen for me.

I was now accompanied solely by a hooker named Donna Vasteynes. She was my birthday present, one that would unwrap itself!

Climbing four flights of stairs to her dimly lit boudoir, I wondered if someone forgot to pay the electric bill for this entire quarter of town. Upon arrival in her modest room, she closed the door firmly behind us, started pulling off her blouse, and asked with a sultry look, "So, Sailor Joe, what you like? Fucky fucky?"

"No, no" I stuttered.

"Ok, Joe, sucky sucky?" she persisted.

"No," I said firmly, having recovered my senses. Clearly, Spanish and not French was her language, so I'd have to improvise; there was too much room here for misunderstandings. "Only they think," I said, pointing towards the bar, then my head, "but not really do," I continued in sign language, waving my hands in broad strokes in the air.

"OK, Joe," she said less energetically.

Now, we waited. "But for how long?" I wondered. "I've never had sex with a woman;

is there an instruction manual? Guide book? Little help here, please," I muttered.

Thirty minutes later she got up from her vanity bench, where she had been applying additional, unnecessary makeup, and motioned towards the door. "Phew, she's done this before," I said to myself with relief, bolting off the bed. Obviously I wasn't the first gay sailor to fall victim to his friends' good intentions.

Reentering the bar, my fellow officers, now even more lubricated with drink, stumbled towards us with jubilant praise for a mission accomplished. And then, she earned her money with an award-worthy performance, rubbing against me, purring my praises: "Sailor Joe, you number one. I love you, Joe." I guessed that this situation must be pretty common, and the clever girls knew how to really make a man feel good—and save his reputation!

I would later feign fond reminiscence of her to my fellow officers in the wardroom. As the legend of my having gotten laid grew, I would refer to her as Miss Panama.

It was certainly *not* because of her beauty—as I recall, she wasn't a great beauty—but in my mind she was a gem because of the stellar performance she had given *them* when she and I had returned to the bar, that night of my birthday.

Our ship left Panama abruptly the next day, and as we pulled away from the shore, I glanced back towards the pier waiting for the *policia* to arrive for me and/or my fellow officers. But we got away, with my reputation glowing.

Once back in the Caribbean Sea, apparently having aborted our plans to pass through the canal to the Pacific Ocean, we made a frighteningly high-speed run for Saint Vincent, where we quickly docked without the requisite use of tug boats. I wondered what our hurry was as I walked toward the gangplank; I needed to go ashore for a VD shot in order to keep up appearances from my birthday night, and out of my naiveté regarding sex with a woman. I also needed tanning lotion for the beach I had hoped to enjoy.

"Sorry, Sir" one of my cute wardroom stewards, who the deck-watch said sternly, "The brow is secured." From the corner of my eye I noted he was wearing his side-arm.

Then what about the four large, very well-built men who were boarding the ship with innumerable hard-sided, silver-colored suit cases? They were allowed on, but I wasn't allowed off?

We had just taken onboard the first four, of eight membered Seal Team Six.

Training for Six had been conducted throughout the United States and abroad, both on military and civilian facilities. Exchange programs and joint trainings had been expanded with the more experienced international teams such as Germany's GSG-9, Great Britain's Special Boat Squadrons (SBS), and France's combat divers.

In all cases, emphasis had been placed on realism in training, in accordance with the "Train as you Fight, Fight as you Train" philosophy popular amongst most of the world's leading special operations and CT units.

These first four members of Seal Team Six, having unpacked enough small weapons to take over a small Third World country, embraced that philosophy while practicing weapons fire on my flight deck. I had nick-named them the Godzilla Quartet because of their physical size and aggressiveness.

When the shooting got out of control, and they shot off our flag staff, I said "I'm not paying for that!" Fortunately with all the noise they were making they couldn't hear me.

I had also been glancing above my helicopter hanger to the Phalanx, which looks like R2-D2 but is in fact a point-defense, total-weapon system consisting of two 20mm gun mounts that provide a terminal defense against incoming air targets. "One push of a button, and I can fire more rounds per minute than the four of you combined," I shouted at them bravely through a cloud of smoke and shell casings.

"What's your classification?" I further challenged them silently. "Mine is Expert – that's one *above* Marksman," I finished with pride, while omitting that in a past skirmish I had chosen to simply run.

On that previous occasion, I had been helping rebuild an orphanage In Nicaragua, when I was suddenly attacked by three Sandinistas. However, it had been three against one and I had to make a split-second, life or death decision. "Do I take out the first two, and risk my life for the third, or do I just realize the odds are against me at this point, and run in order to fight another day?"

Quick thinking had led me to the conclusion that while I would probably have killed the first two of three enemies, the third would have killed me by the time I had reloaded my weapon. No fellow crewmembers were in peril, so I retreated.

Having lived to fight another day, Seal Team Six and I would soon finally be on our way to the beach, but in Grenada. And for this operation all my previous training would be called upon, as well as the ability to take and give orders without question.

But the Godzilla quartet would not be coming back alive.

History would record that four SEALs were lost to drowning in a helicopter insertion offshore during the rescue and evacuation of Governor Sir Paul Scoon.

Hum, yes, well; whichever historian wrote that, needs a new pair of glasses and more ink for his pen.

"United States paratroopers have invaded"

Don't Ask, Do Tell

CHAPTER NINE:
WAR

Mention the tiny Spice Island in the Caribbean—Grenada—to any American who remembers Ronald Reagan's presidency, and the inevitable question you will get is, "Isn't that the county he invaded?"

Grenada had been a source of concern to the Reagan administration for quite some time before I even set foot on the island.

Under the leadership of Prime Minister Maurice Bishop, who came to power in a coup in 1979, the island's government had made a decided turn to the left. Only eight months after taking over, Bishop announced that Cuba would help Grenada build a new airport with a ten-thousand-foot runway, claiming it would be able to accommodate large jetliners and therefore bolster the island's tourist business. What he hadn't said, but was quite apparent, was that the airport would also be able to handle long-range military aircraft.

Shortly after he took office, President Reagan had told Bishop that his ties with Cuba posed a threat to peace in the area.

The first word that a military operation was underway came over Radio Free Grenada, which interspersed programs of reggae music with frantic announcements that the island was being invaded. I was in Combat Systems, for once paying close attention to all the Top Secret message traffic, when I heard:

"United States paratroopers have invaded Grenada with helicopter gunships. Our armed forces have been engaging them in a fierce battle. All Grenadians, report immediately to your respective militia bases. All doctors, nurses, and medics, report to the hospital immediately. The Grenadian people are asked to block all the roads and obstruct the enemy's progress. United States paratroopers have invaded Grenada with helicopter gunships!"

"Look, Bozo," I spoke sarcastically to the radio, "Bonzo wouldn't be here if you hadn't built a landing strip over half your island, then let jets full of Russian weapons land." "What's more," I continued, mimicking towards the radio, "your accent is Russian, not Creole."

I quickly ditched the sarcasm, and stood to attention when I heard Ronald Reagan announce, "Early this morning, forces from six Caribbean democracies and the United States began a landing, or landings (nods, and winks were shared by those of us in Combat Systems because we knew that for twenty-four hours our reconnaissance SEAL team had already been on their island) ...on the island of Grenada in the Eastern Caribbean. We have taken this decisive action for three reasons..."

The Grenada invasion was swift and effective, and I'm proud to say I was part of it. On the Saturday following the invasion—in just one week—all the bad guys had been captured, the Cubans had been sent back to Havana, and Soviet diplomats were ordered to leave the island. An interim government had been formed, and we began our withdrawal.

We gathered in the mess deck to hear the announcement, which was now in a Creole accent, and not Russian. "Grenadians are free. We are thankful to the president of the United States for what he has done for Grenada. At last we are free."

"Praise God, and thanks to Mr. Reagan that we are delivered and we once again are so happy," the voice continued as I developed a grin and shook my head from side to side.

"All in a day's work," I thought, walking calmly away from the radio. However, when I reached the exit hatch from the mess hall, I turned back towards the radio and shouted, "But don't let it happen again, God damn it." Having paused to share a smile with a few of my ship-mates, I continued, "And don't forget my name, William Bonzo; I may want a room with a view of the beach here one day."

What our skipper wanted to do after the battle was to go fishing, this time literally!

With the island still in sight, I stood on the flight deck, ducking from his poor casting abilities, and saw in the distance the ships, planes, and men of our task force heading north like snowbirds from Florida in the spring.

Of course, we were all aware that some people back home weren't in favor of the maneuver; but they didn't have all the information we did. And a month after the invasion, *Time* magazine would describe it as having had "broad popular support."

A congressional study group would conclude that the invasion had been justified. It was thought that U.S. students at the Grenada University near a contested runway could have been taken hostage as U.S. diplomats in Iran had been four years previously.

The group's report would cause House Speaker Tip O'Neill to change his position on the issue from opposition to support.

However, some members of the study group would dissent from its findings. Congressman Louis Stokes would state: "Not a single American national was in any way placed in danger or placed in a hostage situation prior to the invasion."

The Congressional Black Caucus would denounce the invasion, and seven Democratic congressmen, led by Ted Weiss, would introduce a quixotic resolution to impeach Reagan... which would go, of course, exactly nowhere.

"...seemed like an eternity in hell."

Don't Ask, Do Tell

CHAPTER TEN:
LAND HO!

That was exactly where I'd be going next too – nowhere, at least figuratively. What's more all the training the military had previously invested in me would languish as I was thrown into a personal battle.

After the war in the Caribbean, I had a tour of duty in Guantanamo Bay, Cuba where I was gassed, shot at, and up to my neck in seawater from a flooding compartment.

While this vignette could take an entire chapter itself to tell, I already feel the breath of the military on my neck, and sense their frown at the morsel I have just told.

I will tell you that the military policy regarding hair length "…should not interfere with the proper wearing of military head gear" does *not* refer to uniform hats that try to hold on to a Marine's shaved head during a parade. It refers to situations such as mine, when I was in a room when a canister of nerve gas was tossed through the window, exploding its contents. Only a tight seal on my gas mask, not possible if I were sporting shoulder length blond hair, would save me.

The short, impressionistic scene was inserted here because it happened to me, and is part of my character. The military is not just holding hands in the shower, baking soufflés and singing *Anchor's Away*.

Nor are all battles fought with guns and ammunition.

After Grenada, and after Cuba, I was back in Florida – alive – where I took the cover off my Mercedes in storage at Mayport and told her, "Let's go girl, it's just me and you."

While I loved going to sea, and relished the thought of crossing the North Atlantic where many of our ships and service members were being sent because of the tensions in the Middle East, I had orders to Roosevelt Field on Long Island, in New York.

WTF??? This was the very same antiquated airfield first used by Charles Lindbergh! God damn it to hell...well, at least I would be able to see the ocean from Long Island.

Just before Mercedes and I crossed the border into Georgia, I stopped for fuel, and took one last look at my orders to ensure they said New York, and not New Guinea, or New Zealand, or new anything besides New York.

The filling station attendant said slowly, while scratching his five-o-clock shadow – Greenwich Mean Time—judging from its length, "Yes, son, there are two kinds of people who live in the sunshine state..." he drawled as if he was about to launch into *Swanee River* while eyeing my *German-made* Mercedes.

I had braced myself to hear "…and we don't take a shine to any queers" when I finally heard the end of his southern idiom "We got newlyweds, and nearly deads."

Wanting to bond with him, and prevent myself from hearing any "queer" slurs, I shared how my own uncle had driven his *American-made* Cadillac into a telephone pole in Clearwater, Florida, after having suffered a heart attack and that yep, my happily-married sister lived in Pompano Beach, Florida.

Having passed my manhood test, I continued my drive north with the filling station attendant, my life in Florida, and Ensign Fisher and his girlfriend in my rear view mirror.

The urge to be me, to be free, to stop hiding that I was gay, and the longing for one special relationship with another man was now about to be compounded with being confined for two years to land, surrounded by people who could think only of themselves and not the needs of the group.

I arrived in New York, and was impressed by the housing arrangements at Mitchel Field, next to Roosevelt Field on Long Island. There was row upon row of old growth tree-lined streets with five thousand-square foot, three-story Colonial mansions where the officers lived.

I looked at it all, awestruck, thinking this might not be so bad after all, and wondering how long it would take me to paint the inside of mine! One does want some color, *non*?

But, oh no, then I learned that in order to live in one of these you had to be married! I on the other hand, got a ten-foot by ten-foot cinder block room at Fort Totten in the outer borough of Queens.

It had linoleum floors, bad plumbing, and no cooking facilities – let alone the eat-in kitchen, hard wood floors and formal dining room of the mansions at Mitchel Field. Why not just send me to jail, I thought while taking in my new surroundings. It would have a similar décor, but at least there I would get served breakfast, lunch and dinner!

Cheer up, I tried to encourage myself, because I knew that at this very moment there were men at sea hot-bunking it. This means that when there were not enough bunks for each crewmember to have his own, they shared. In this bizarre arrangement, three sailors, each in a different watch section, shared a single rack. It was entertaining to contemplate what would happen if one was a bit late crawling out of bed and the next was a bit early?

I decided to make the best of this situation, and realizing the proximity of Fort Totten to Manhattan I became excited at the prospect of all that the big city had to offer.

In my free time, I would take the subway to Times Square and get free tickets to Broadway, and to off-Broadway, sometimes *way off* Broadway, shows from the USO (United Services Organization).

Not fully acclimated to civilians, I chose to work out at the Marine Corps base in Garden City, where I could be among my own. In between sets on the bench press, I was stretching and enjoying the sun that languished over the abandoned railroad platform at the rear of the base gym. It's then that I met the teenaged son of a serviceman—one of those lucky marrieds who had landed a house at Mitchel Field— who was overseas. We became friends in the manner of my other friendships in the military: platonic.

After a few months, in addition to working out together every day David would take me to his parents' house at Mitchel Field for dinner, a routine which soon became a nightly ritual.

His mother was happy that her fatherless son had someone to look up to, and help him with his school work. Yet while this wasn't exactly the relationship I was looking for, I enjoyed being part of this family; plus the food was great!

Having two weeks leave, I invited him to go with me to my aunt and uncle's cabin in Canada. We talked a lot to each other during the over five hundred mile drive from New York, to Eagle Lake, Ontario. Just guy stuff, like our gym workout progress and goals...his school work...and how I couldn't wait to jump into Eagle Lake!

Steering my Mercedes off the hard pavement of The Queen's Highway, we proceeded the final fifty miles on a dirt road – barely noticing the difference from the comfort of my German made machine.

The first thing we saw upon arrival at the cabin was my uncle's empty boat trailer that meant one thing – the twenty-two foot, wood hulled, twin-engine Chris-Craft Sportsman was in the water and waiting for us to enjoy!

We didn't waste a second getting onto the lake, completely forgetting the twelve hour drive from New York.

My Aunt Ruth was driving the boat while waving at all the neighbors on the lakeside, oblivious to the fact that David and I were tethered to it, trying to stay erect on our skis in the chop created by her erratic navigation each time she saw an acquaintance! Eventually we both surrendered and dove into the water.

Now, while water skiing had about as much chance of getting into the Olympics as did NASCAR, my Uncle Dale in turn gave an award worthy performance that showed David and I how it was done! He finished his tour-de-lac by letting go of the rope, gliding towards shore, discarding one ski, then the other, and walked out of the lake – all without even getting wet above the knees!

After dinner, cooked as evenly as I could on a wood burning stove, and eaten alfresco under the crisp, clear Canadian sky, David and I went happily together to chop wood, and light the fire for my family's traditional evening sauna in the bath house by the lake.

The entire family would arrive, sit around and sweat, while talking story, then run and jump in the frigid lake water – owe! I was proud of how my family had so readily accepted David into the fold, and equally happy how quickly David had taken to them. Although, the excessive amount of water David poured onto the hot bath house stones was grounds for dismissal from the tribe.

On the tree lined ridge above the cabins, lived a family by the name of Pace. They occupied a large, old farmhouse which was adjacent to an abandoned barn that they had converted into a sort of huge fun room. All of us campers were invited to use the barn at our leisure.

David and I would swing like monkeys on the thick, burlap ropes suspended from massive twelve inch square ceiling beams. Landing with a thump on antique over-stuffed sofas, we'd quickly repeat, over and over to the point of exhaustion, our pretended auditions for the *Cirque de Soleil*.

On the few occasions that we elders would take the boat across the lake for provisions, David would mind the fort.

He became particularly fond of my six year old nephew. Those two rascals could play, and wrestle in the dirt from sunrise to sauna time. I clearly remember David standing on the dock, shirtless, buff and tan, holding my half shrieking, half laughing nephew around the waist with one arm over the water and threatening to let go. David was now a part of *my* family.

This was heaven on earth, and one of the happiest times of my life. Yet, two weeks passed in the blink of an eye, and it was back to New York.

I was thoroughly enjoying the delights of New York, between the free theater tickets, the feeling of something always happening, and the perks of life in a beautiful city – and having a friend like David.

Jogging around Central Park was invigorating, both for its physical exertion, and for the atmosphere. I was totally charmed by the brownstones, all full of various lives and their stories. I wished I could know all the inhabitants, maybe even one special, intimate one, but that wish, among so many to date, would be cut short by the military.

Of course, it hadn't been all jogging in Central Park and going to shows. While stationed on

Long Island, I was the Officer in Charge of the military Commissary. I was in charge of twenty-five military personnel, and fifty civilians.

One civilian employee wasn't working at par, and eventually, I had her removed from her position, not knowing that this would ignite a firestorm against me.

This employee named Toni in turn threw every charge in the book at me, hoping that one of her allegations would stick. She filed suit against me with the Navy Review Board, and in the suit she alleged everything from Communism to Fascism. That she accused me of being Communist because I quoted Karl Marx was laughable; that she accused me of Fascism because I liked Italian food and art was ludicrous.

But one of the allegations, of course, was that I was gay, and that was different, because it was true. Not that I'd acted on it. Still, after years serving our country, sharing quarters with other officers, ensuring my men had food to eat and, when times were tough, films to watch and Christmas gifts to open, I had not ever engaged in sexual activity with another man.

And yet, I was undeniably gay. There was no way I could pretend to myself that my interest was in women—despite having faked it with the prostitute in Panama.

Perhaps most hurtful, Toni accused me of being sexually involved with David.

The day of the tribunal was one of the worst of my life. We met formally in a conference room at the Navy Base, Brooklyn at 1300 hours. There passed three hours of my sitting there, listening to her accusations, watching as she was questioned, and then taking the stand myself.

"She said I was un-American because I liked the New York Yankees instead of the Brooklyn Dodgers?" I questioned them right back. "With people like her in Brooklyn, no wonder the Dodgers moved to Los Angeles" I said in mock defense to the Review Board members, my having already decided that I was going to be found guilty regardless of my innocence.

When they got to the point of questioning me about my sexuality, I felt my blood boil. "None of your eff-ing business," I wanted to say, but of course I held back. The only gay activity I had pursued to date was looking at magazines in the privacy of my quarters at Fort Totten or while on one of my mini vacations far away from the military.

Instead, I was honest, informing them that I had never engaged in sexual activity with another man, or boy. It was fortunate that the truth was nothing to be afraid of.

Towards the end of that long day, I was awaiting their findings for yet another hour in the stifling, windowless hallway. My attorney, a female officer and attorney from the JAG (Navy Judge Advocate General) office exited the conference room slowly, sat next to me gently, and informed me with tears that all charges were dismissed. I honestly didn't know why she was crying, or what she was feeling.

However my feelings toward the military had changed irrevocably.

The grudge the disgruntled employee carried and vendetta she had gone on would eventually contribute to the end of my career— the military forgets, and forgives, nothing – even lies.

While I had had a great life in the Navy, and endured hardships, the short time that passed while being stationed in New York, and especially in that military courtroom, seemed like an eternity in hell.

What's more, call it my European discretion if you must, I believe that sometimes in order to understand what's being said, that you must also listen to what's *not* being said. This applies to the remainder of what I feel about those dark days in New York.

Let's move on to happier times for now, yeah? And I don't just mean the Yankees in the World Series!

"I wonder how much
I can tell...without the
Department of Defense
arresting me"

Don't Ask, Do Tell

CHAPTER ELEVEN:
MOVING FORWARD

Moving forward will be more recent actions in the Med and the Gulf. I wonder, how much can I tell, yet get published without the Department of Defense banning the book, or arresting me, or...?

After the tribunal, I was more than ready to leave New York. Having sold my Mercedes, my one constant friend, bid farewell to David and his mother, I looked forward, not knowing how long I'd be gone or even if I'd make it back alive.

I was enroute via commercial air to my ship in Mayport, Florida – hopefully I wouldn't get lost like my yet unknown friend RN3 (Radioman Third Class) Steven Gray would while trying to get to his ship the USS *Texas* (CGN39). Both of us would be bound for the Persian Gulf.

The baggage handler at the Atlanta airport taught me another southern idiom. I shivered slightly when he said "Yes, son, when we die, and we all most certainly will die, on our way to heaven there is a connecting flight in Atlanta."

I felt sick, either from fear of dying, or the grits I had had for breakfast, so bee-lined it for the john.

Imagine me sitting in the john at the Atlanta airport, with my pants down around my ankles, reading more poetry of the South such as "While sitting here reading, this shit house art, I suddenly let loose a tremendous fart. It shook the ceiling and burst the walls, and burned all the hair off of my mother %&*$ing balls."

Well folks, I've delayed it long enough so at the risk of my getting arrested, I'm going to proceed with this story and tell you about my Mediterranean and Persian Gulf cruise. Anyone afraid of being exposed (to classified information, my dears) *put down the book now* and run away.

However, exposure to crewmen in nothing more than wet boxer-briefs, with bare chests, young and full of life does occur on this trip and while it won't get us arrested, as a gay man I will need to be a bit more careful.

Please understand I had resolved to keep any of these thoughts to myself.

I arrived in Mayport, and with pants up and head down, read the ship's orders which were exactly two words "Meander East."

The *Titanic* sank during dead calm seas, but our less than certain route would take us through a gale storm in the North Atlantic – yippee!

On this voyage, all officers were called upon to command the ship in turn, as the skipper seemed to be spending an inordinate amount of time in

Combat Systems reading an increased stream of Top Secret messages. I interrupted him once, bringing him his coffee, and asked rhetorically if my recipe for Quiche Lorraine was among the papers he was shuffling through. He gave me a quick, if not nervous smile.

I had the bridge. "Was it dot dot dot, dash dash dash dash, dot dot dot, or vice versa?" I asked myself, rehearsing for our potential need to use the Morse code distress signal first used by the Titanic.

Slam, splash…*Slam*, splash…First the bow of the ship slammed into the ocean, then deep green water splashed on the bridge windows. *Slam*, splash…as the forward missile launcher now disappeared below the surface of the water, and aft the twin propulsion screws flew into the air—"God I love this job," I said to no one in particular.

Above me, spanning the breadth of the bridge was a rail not used for hanging laundry, but for hanging onto for your life! "Come right forty-five degrees," I sang out, both my feet off the deck as I firmly gripped the bridge rail. We needed to get out of this storm, or the captain would be wearing dinner, and I'd get a reputation for being a food slinger.

The ship calmed down on our new course, and I could breathe and stand firmly on the deck, looking so handsome in my three-quarter-length bridge coat. I saw what looked like a book of matches on the deck, picked it up, and placed it in my coat pocket for disposal later. This skipper liked things clean and tidy, and I thought smugly, "We'll get along!"

The very next morning the First Officer entered my cabin, no doubt to thank me for maneuvering the ship out of danger the previous night. "May I see your bridge coat?" he said sternly.

"Sure," I said eagerly, thinking, "he needs to measure it for a new, additional stripe."

He went right to the pocket, pulled out the matchbook, and said, "What's this?" Without waiting for my response, he opened it, revealing thin sheets of paper.

"Dunno, Sir. I found it on the bridge last night and was gonna trash it, just as soon as I saved the ship and our lives," I said remarkably.

"It's paraphernalia," he snapped, looking me square in the eyes.

"What's that?" I said without hesitation.

Now, he had to make a quick judgment: Was I trafficking drugs in the middle of the North Atlantic, or incredibly naïve regarding them? He chose the latter, which was the truth, and soon after made me Officer in Charge of drug enforcement on the ship.

To this day, I can't remember for the life of me who all was on the bridge that night, nor which one of those little pot-smoking jerks might have pointed the finger at me in order to protect themselves.

When at sea for lengths of time, eating was important to crew morale. Unfortunately we had gotten underway without a ship's baker. I negotiated with our rotund skipper to be the baker on this cruise, as long as I didn't have to drive the ship anymore. He agreed rapidly, licking his chops and downing a Dramamine. And by the way, the ship's baker on the ill-fated *Titanic* survived*!*

Mind you, I still had all my other duties, such as Mess Officer, Disbursing Officer, and Laundry Officer for the crew. Great! I fed them, gave them their allowance, and cleaned their clothes – I always wanted to be a mother!

I was also the Helicopter Control Officer. Since we had gotten underway with only one helicopter, yet had two hangars (were we in a hurry, or what?), I converted one hangar into a gym for the crew (and me). Additionally when there were no flight ops, the flight deck became Steel Beach, but we'll get back to that—let's eat!

It was now just after two o'clock in the morning in the cold North Atlantic Ocean, exactly the hour when the *Titanic* finally succumbed to her wounds. The moon above me was shining onto the mirror-like, calm ocean as if it was a Broadway premiere beacon, so "I guess we won't hit anything like they did," I sighed comfortably standing on our flight deck, the hanger door opened, the ocean view gym awaiting me.

Sliding happily down the ladder, deep into the galley, I mixed the dough and let it rise while I went to work out in my gym.

Returning to the galley, I now cut the dough and let it rise once more while I showered. Finally I returned to the galley to finish building my masterpieces of fresh baguettes, doughnuts, and pastries, and waited for my boys to succumb. Interrupting my vision, into the galley at 0500 hours rolled my rotund skipper, unable to resist until breakfast was served in the wardroom—what a wake-up call his figure was! He was obviously unaware we now had a gym onboard.

However, good things come to those who wait, and what good figures I would see later that day on our "Steel Beach" which is what we called the flight deck, turned beach, sans sand. Crewmembers swam in the ocean in what they had—white cotton boxers. Add water, and you had a delicious recipe!

Days later, during flight operations on that very same Steel Beach, with a shot of adrenalin I noticed the fuel hatch on our Seahawk helicopter was open. No big deal if it had been on your Ford Ranger; however, on this sophisticated piece of military equipment, something as small as a fuel hatch, no more than four inches square, if detached from the craft and sucked into the engines, could have brought it crashing onto the deck. As Helicopter Control Officer, I brought the craft down, we closed the gas cap, and away she went on her mission. It was all in a day's work to me.

The military thought otherwise, and the Admiral himself congratulated me with the nomination letter for pro of the week. I say nomination because I *didn't win!* I saved numerous lives and prevented the loss of a multimillion-dollar helicopter, perhaps even our ship if the craft had crashed and burned on deck, and I *didn't win!*

Even though this insult—not being what I felt was properly recognized for something I'd done—had nothing to do with being gay, at that moment, the anger I'd been penting up all those years, the frustration with hiding who I was, spilled out, and right to the Admiral's face I responded, "What does it take to win an award in the military? Whose dick do I have to suck?"

And I didn't leave it at that, almost as if I wanted to come out – even though, of course, I didn't. "Could I at least have some of the thousand pairs of Imelda's shoes that were left in the palace in Manila?" I went on, "especially since she got a free ride on a US helicopter?"

He shook his head, and did not respond. I had, after all, been dating his daughter Anna, albeit by mail and on the few occasions I actually had my feet on dry land in Mayport, since being introduced to her by my cousin Lieutenant Commander Carter.

She had, and continued to be the perfect foil. I like to think we both got something out of it, as she seemed prim and old-fashioned, and I doubt she was interested in men. As for me, with her as my date, I was now protected from anyone pointing a finger at me again and accusing me of being gay.

As our battle group continued to meander east, we encountered an underway replenishment ship. She had brought us fuel, food, and, yippee – the latest movies to trade! But, I had to go get them. For my crew, I would do it.

This was a connected replenishment, which is two or more ships steaming side-by-side. The hoses and lines used to transfer fuel, ammunition, supplies, and personnel connected the ships.

"You want me to go *where*, on *what*?" I said, wide-eyed, to our skipper on the gun deck as I made damned sure my life-jacket straps were tightened to the point of cutting off blood circulation. No, they weren't going to stuff me into a gun turret and fire, although that may have been preferable to what I was about to experience. "I'm over two hundred pounds, and that rope is half an inch thick," I tried to reason. "You go first!" I suggested with a smile to the Captain.

And sure enough, as fast as Willie the Coyote, the First Officer was half an inch from my face, shouting, "You get on that rope soldier."

"I'm a sailor, you moron," I mumbled in a daze as I slammed into the solid steel side of the ship that had been keeping pace alongside us. I shook it off while mouthing back towards my ship, "Way to go, guys, trying to kill me after all I've done for you in the past."

I made my way below decks, two feet and two hands on the ladder, sliding down ten feet in a second while letting out a "Yippee!" Hey, what did I have to lose with the stunt? The near-death rope ride had already proven I was immortal.

"I'm trading you these movies for your crew," I said to the neighboring Supply Officer. "The officers can play with themselves in the wardroom for all I care."

He laughed knowingly and said, "What do want in exchange?"

"One thousand two hundred and twenty pairs of shoes?" I laughed back at him.

"Are you still dating the Admiral's daughter?" he asked abruptly, so as to quickly distance the conversation from a man wanting ladies shoes.

"Yep," I replied equally abruptly.

For emphasis I continued, "Yes, we still use the Admiral's cottage at Jacksonville Beach—I love the beach!" I said. "Our weekends there, by the fire after a long day in the water are like being in heaven."

Now standing, grasping the movies I had traded, I finished our transaction with a surreptitious glance to see if he was buying my cover story.

These personal skirmishes to prove my manhood would continue throughout my military career, to the point that sometimes I wished for what no sailor or soldier wished for–to die in combat.

"For crying out loud," I wanted to scream, "I'm not the enemy!" Sometimes I wished I hadn't run in Nicaragua, and had been shot. "I wish the line that is tethering me between ships would snap and deposit my lifeless body in my beloved ocean" I pleaded to no one as I sailed back towards my ship. "You see that 'Battle E' painted on the side of our ship?" I wanted to say as I made my way back onboard, not allowing myself to drop, "I helped you earn it – me, the homo!"

Arriving back on our gun deck, alive, I was greeted silently by our First Officer, his steely blue eyes burning a hole right through me. "What, are you sorry I made it back alive?" I asked right back, silently. "You better just lighten up," I continued our wordless dialogue, "or the next port we pull into, I'll tell everyone in Russian that you have a thing for Rudolf

Nureyev." I was bluffing, of course. My sense of humor was just my constant companion and unbiased friend.

Our First Officer was a good man who I held in the highest regard. It was not his choice, but his genetics that he was tall, with blond hair and steely blue eyes. His occasional goose step, on the other hand, gave me reason to pause.

Once when I had been summoned to his Stateroom I imagined I'd hear him singing "Deutschland, Deutschland über alles, über alles in der Welt." I smiled when I heard through his cabin door *Anchors Aweigh* (the 1906 version):

Stand Navy out to sea, fight our battle cry,

We'll never change our course, so vicious foe steer shy-y-y-y.

Roll out the TNT, anchors aweigh,

Sail on to victory and sink their bones to Davy Jones, hooray!

Anchors away, my boys, anchors aweigh,

Farewell to foreign shores, we sail at break of day-ay-ay-ay.

Through our last night on shore, drink to the foam,

Until we meet once more, here's wishing you a happy voyage home.

Blue of the Mighty Deep, gold of god's sun,

Let these colors be till all of time be done, done, done.

On seven seas we learn, Navy's stern call,

Faith, courage, service true, with honor, over honor, over all.

It gave me goose bumps standing in the passage way outside his cabin, hearing that song again, having sung it many times in the Navy Choir at Supply Corps School in Athens.

So before entering his cabin, I strengthened my resolve to serve my country and burry *any* personal thoughts that may have tried to find their way to the surface throughout the cruise, where over two hundred men had been confined to living and working in close quarters for months on end.

We still had a mission to accomplish, even though the skipper had remained silent on its details. It was our duty to follow his command, and as officer on his ship I had to set the example for others to follow – and thoughts of having sex, or even an intimate, quiet moment alone with one of the men was *not* the right example.

It hurt me, because I sincerely cared about

the welfare of my men. And the arms-length I had to put between us was, I knew, for the entire unit's well being for whatever duty would call.

"Tovarisch, you saw something?"

Don't Ask, Do Tell

CHAPTER TWELVE:
THE OLD WORLD, BUT IT'S NEW TO ME!

Having crossed the North Atlantic in a gale, saved the ship from sinking, prevented the loss of our aircraft because someone forgot to close the gas cap, and survived attempted murder by drowning for the sake of a film festival, I pinched my arm to ensure the islands we were now rapidly approaching were real, and not part of a continuing dream.

The Azores is a Portuguese archipelago in the Atlantic Ocean about 1,500 kilometers (930 miles) from Lisbon and about 3,900 kilometers (2,400 miles) from the east coast of North America.

It was the first land we, and Christopher Columbus by the way, sighted after crossing the Atlantic.

He had stopped here after his 1493 voyage to America. After being mistaken for a pirate, he was taken prisoner and was only set free after officials justified his landing.

"Hey, we just want some gas," I shouted, and waved a friendly hand to the two ominous persons I saw sitting on the jetty at the entrance to the harbor. They were looking directly at me.

"I wonder what the food is like in Portuguese prisons," I continued in muffled tones.

Our skipper must have known about their hospitality as well, because no sooner than the gas cap was closed on our ship we were steaming towards the Strait of Gibraltar, which connects the Atlantic Ocean to the Mediterranean Sea.

"Call me," I mimicked towards the two figures on the jetty below with my hand held at my ear and mouth. "Let's do lunch" I persisted bravely from the safety of our flight deck, the Azores vanishing quickly from sight.

The narrow strait separates Europe and Africa by only 7.7 nautical miles, making it a real navigational challenge. I was just glad I wasn't driving the boat, because it was a genuine geographical tight squeeze!

Once through the strait, just like when a garden hose has been squeezed tightly causing water to shoot out at high velocity, we shot out of it and into the Mediterranean Sea. I barely had time to get a good look at the Rock of Gibraltar, which is the Spanish derivation of the Arabic name Jabal Tariq, meaning "Mountain of Tariq."

There was a Russian anchorage off the coast of Libya that we breezed boldly through at full throttle early one morning.

The Russian ships impressed me. One was a massive Kiev Class, 273 meters (896 feet) long, a beam of 32.6 meters (107 feet) with eight boilers and four turbines. She could do up to 59 km (32 knots) and carried 1,600 men.

Imagine its skipper on his bridge at the crack of dawn, his ship motionless at anchor. While drinking his vodka-laced coffee and surveying the sea, suddenly, and out of nowhere, a United States guided missile cruiser went by at seemingly 40 knots. He probably had turned to his First Officer and said, "Tovarich, you saw something?"

Simultaneously I had been on that blur of a cruiser he was staring at open-jawed, shouting towards my bridge, "Slow down, God damn it! I want to get a better look!"

Continuing our mad-dash, we made a bee-line for Port Said, and then steered through the Suez Canal.

"Honestly, if this whole trip is going to be rushing here, rushing there, then just let me off the ship," I shrugged.

And that is *exactly* what they would do.

Unlike the Panama Canal, which is a series of cement locks that raise and lower ships as they pass over different elevations on the Isthmus of Panama, the Suez Canal is basically a long ditch in the sand with sea water flowing freely.

Passing through the canal with half sunken casualties of war that littered the sandy banks, we stopped in Djibouti, a country in the Horn of Africa on the Gulf Aden. The skipper and the entire crew remained onboard, déjà vu, with the "engine still running" while I went ashore for more supplies. "That's an awful lot of supplies we've been getting recently," I puzzled.

"What are we *really* picking up?" I wondered as I stood on the pier, having followed orders and simply signed for the crates. While glancing at them being loaded on our ship, I drank a Pepsi, looking intently at the bottle and trying to decipher it's Arabic lettering.

While the ship remained in Djibouti, I would fly to Manama, Bahrain: Try saying that three times fast and you'll sound like you speak Farsi, too.

I was going to arrange for the usual food, fuel and ship-to-shore service. "Couldn't we have called ahead?" I thought.

"Manama was mentioned in Islamic chronicles at least as far back as the year 1345," I was reading from the guide book clutched in my left hand, "and was conquered by Portugal in 1521, then by Persians in 1602. Since 1783 it has been under the control of the Al-Khalifa dynasty," I continued reading while my right hand strongly grasped the edge of the tiny skiff that was being piloted by a man wearing a colorful headdress, and was rapidly and dangerously taking me ashore from the platform I had landed on.

"Manama was declared a free port in 1958, and in 1971 it became the capital of independent Bahrain," I finished, looking up from the book, having arrived onshore, and feeling totally out-of-my element and abandoned.

In short, Manama is one of those tiny countries most Americans have never heard of; even in the crash course in Middle Eastern geography that Americans have gotten in the past ten years, a place like Manama doesn't register, even though it's been around since the Middle Ages.

"Hey, dammit," I said, walking down the gang plank from the skiff towards the pier while shaking my fist at my skipper on our ship on the *other* side of Saudi Arabia. "I speak French, German, Italian, and *nim noga* Russian, but not bloody Farsi!" A good thing he couldn't really hear me, I calculated the distance between us. I remembered how he had nervously waved his hand back at me when I had been thrown off the ship in Egypt.

I was about to get a crash course in using *my* hands to communicate and I projected it would look good on my resume; if I survived.

I was also going to the local bank, if you could call Omar's Exchange a bank, and get dinars for our crew to use as currency while in port. We were strongly discouraged from using U.S. dollars, even though they went *much* farther with the gold vendors. I wondered if this was where Big Daddy Kane, or Salt-N-Pepa had shopped?

I discovered a large ex-pat British community in Bahrain, even though I didn't remember reading about this place having been a British colony. A steakhouse with great western food was a refuge, and my umbilical cord. Having there met and befriended two British naval officers, I commented on their dining etiquette. It was far superior to that of my fellow officers who didn't know the difference between a salad fork, and a pitch fork!

Once I returned to my ship, alive, and with camel dung on my shoes we left port in Djibouti. Frankly I was surprised that we actually had had time to slow down and smell the local culture. I was just starting to understand it and wanted to learn more.

Now, for your safety and mine, I'm not yet going to tell you where we went next, nor what we did thereabouts. The military does make us sign a confidentiality agreement upon separation from the service.

However, I can tell you that I was anxious and pensive as we steamed through the Strait of Hormuz. Located between Oman and Iran, the Strait connects the Persian Gulf with the Gulf of Oman and the Arabian Sea.

My anxiety came from advanced knowledge that this area had been mined, and ships were getting their bottoms blown out.

My pensiveness was from my very personal experience. While stationed in New York

I had also been the Casualty Assistance Calls Officer.

While standing on the deck of my ship entering the Persian Gulf, I pulled from my saddest of memories during that previous, dark part of my life and career.

I knew that somewhere in America, as a result of our involvement in the Middle East, a door was being knocked on. A shocked and grieving family member would hear the same words that I had also recited "On behalf of a grateful nation, it is my duty to inform you of the loss of your…"

I survived the Arabian Sea, obviously, earning an Armed Forces Expeditionary Medal for the, well – expedition.

While our orders had been vaguely to meander east, the journey we had undertaken had been for a very specific purpose; exploration and research. That would explain why I had had to surrender one of my largest onboard storerooms for crates of "research gear." And, it was twice now, that I had preceded the actual battle for "exploration" and why much of my story is still clouded in secrecy.

A friend I would make years later, after we were both out of the military, RN3 Steven Gray (Radioman Third Class), would participate in the actual fight during Operation Desert Storm. Well, after he finally got to his ship the USS *Texas* (CGN39).

He had been in Alameda when he got his orders to report to the *Texas*, which was in Japan. On a commercial flight to meet the *Texas*, he met some girls. Well, boys will be boys, and in Japan he missed his ship that had already sailed with the *Nimitz* battle group, steaming for the Persian Gulf.

He would reach the *Texas* just before she passed through the Strait of Hormuz, and unlike my earlier horizontal wire act, he would do a VERTREP; or simply said, the same wire transfer of personnel, but vertically from a helicopter.

Once onboard, and in the midst of the fighting, the other half of his two-man team in the radio shack would inform him he was gay. Now, you already know Steven liked girls, enough to cause him to miss his ship, but his simple response was "OK." Combat readiness had not been diminished. The effort that might have been spent on ambiguity was now better used for the mission.

Their duty in the Gulf done, they would both earn a Bronze Star. Apparently having an openly gay man, serving right next to a straight man had absolutely no direct or deleterious impact on their combat readiness! In fact, the straight forward honesty the two men shared gave them a bond that had made them a *more* effective, even award winning team.

On *my* way out of the Persian Gulf, my sexual identity still a secret, my ship made a swing through the Indian Ocean and made a stop at Diego Garcia, a tiny, remote island similar to Napoleon's Elba. However we and specifically *moi* (phew!), weren't going to be marooned ashore there: we just stopped for some ice cream.

Stop laughing, I'm serious, dammit! I'm not making this stuff up, I'm not that clever.

Diego Garcia is located in the Indian Ocean about 1,600 km (1,000 miles) south of the southern coast of India, and the closest other countries are Sri Lanka and Maldives. "You should have sent Napoleon here," I mouthed in the air to no one in particular as I stood on deck remarking in our isolation, "and then he wouldn't have escaped!"

In the 1960s, the encompassing Chagos archipelago was secretly leased to the United Kingdom and detached from Mauritius with the intention of expelling its entire population and establishing a military base; and I thought British colonialism was dead?

In 1971 the United Kingdom and the United States had entered an agreement under which the latter would set up a military base in Diego Garcia. "Oh, sure, blame the removal of indigenous people on us," I muttered as its shore loomed before us.

Still, I was intrigued by this rock. For some unknown reason, I had a sense of expectation.

Yet after only five seconds ashore, it was to me just one of the many U.S. military bases scattered around the world on remote islands. Regardless of its intriguing history, the island was now simply being used as a naval refueling and support station.

Although human-rights groups claimed it was used by the U.S. government for the "controversial extraordinary rendition of prisoners."

"Golly, saying that's a mouthful," I said stretching my jaw, having repeated their claims to the crewmember who had become my escort ashore. I was also listening to my stomach growl, and feeling sweat pouring down the back of my khakis. "What I could use is a mouthful of ice cream on this blistering, hot day..."

And voila! What the island had in addition to a gas station was cows – lots of them! Plus it had a full-fledged dairy that made, yep: *ice cream.*

The island's lesser known fame was abundant grasslands that were perfect for raising cattle. And what are cattle perfect for but producing milk, and what's milk perfect for but making ice cream! That's right; this remote outpost had terrific ice cream. Now this is one expedition I would savor!

As usual, I was thrust to the forefront – and in this case into the hands of now-Lieutenant

Shawn Baker, who I remembered immediately from our days together in training in Athens, Georgia. It turned out he had been stationed here for the past year, in perfect timing for us to bump into each other in the requisition room.

Recovering from the shock of seeing him again, with his hands now lingering around mine I said "What the hell happened to your hair?"

He gave me that beautiful, side-ways smile I had loved so many years earlier and said "I've been marooned here, milking cows."

"And your six-pack abs?" I continued, looking at his now rotund figure.

"Hey, I only have only cows to look at me now – not you" he said in a low voice, pulling me closer while surveying my escort for any response. He was still brave, and a flirt; I smiled secretly to myself during his embrace, which I ended by handing him a requisition form.

Meantime, the ice cream was loaded onto the ship while she was being refueled.

Arriving back dockside, what did I see but my ship, moving away from the shore, becoming smaller and smaller. They had left port without me, smiling with two hundred gallons of fresh, creamy, homemade ice cream onboard.

"I like Rocky Road," I shouted from the pier as the ship disappeared on the horizon—*without me!*

Now I knew what Napoleon and Gilligan felt like. "Oh well, if I'm going to die here at least I'll die happy with all this *ice cream!*" and Shawn.

I continued shouting towards the silhouette on the horizon that was my ship. Recovering quickly from having been marooned, I considered my lunch options. "This place was conquered, sorry I mean 'rented' by the British," I discussed with my two imaginary castaways, "so there must be a decent place to get afternoon tea."

Afternoon tea is often a misnomer, some referring to it as high tea because it sounds lofty and regal when in fact in Britain it is the "meat tea" or dinner.

This raises the question of what is low tea, a sandwich from the 7-11? American hotels continue to misunderstand and offer tidbits of fancy pastries and cakes on delicate china.

Once I went to afternoon tea at a Ritz Carlton, and having gotten sticker shock from the bill blurted out "At these prices, do I get to keep the china?"

Obviously, I thought, I was becoming delirious form the heat on Diego Garcia. And delusional, I continued while staggering for a place to sit on the pier – I could have sworn I met Shawn Baker again!?

"On behalf of Her Majesty the Queen, may I welcome you onboard?"

Don't Ask, Do Tell

CHAPTER THIRTEEN: HELP? HELP? ANYONE?

The ungrateful bastards: I had loaded the ship with fresh ice cream, milk, the latest cinema releases, and they left without me.

Unbeknownst to me, The Department of Defense had entered into numerous agreements with its allies, coalition partners and friendly foreign countries to allow for the exchange or assignment of foreign personnel to U.S. defense establishments, with corresponding assignments to theirs. It was *not* to be used for exchanging technical data or software related to the design, development, manufacture or operation of military systems.

In other words, the U.S. could trade an officer with Great Britain, for example, and that's exactly what they'd done with me.

Now standing on the pier, fanning myself with my white navy gloves, looking sheepishly left, right, and then left, I mouthed "Help, help..."

Suddenly I heard "Lefttenant Bonzo?"

"Guilty" I reacted.

"On behalf of Her Majesty the Queen, may I welcome you onboard...?" a well-manicured man in uniform said with precision.

"Yippee, the HMS *Queen Elizabeth II* is in port? Is the queen onboard? Can we go for afternoon tea?" I rambled excitedly.

I had been exchanged, how rude. What prisoner had America gotten in return, I wondered. And I hoped the British didn't expect me to give them *any* information *or* ice cream.

Well, I got neither tea, nor was I on her majesty's cruise ship. I was on one of her naval ships, and the Pommies drank beer, not English Breakfast, on their combat ships.

What's more, their skipper, one of the two British officers I had befriended and charmed in Bahrain, had a small electronic piano in the stateroom of his British destroyer. The instrument would be transported to their mess deck on Sundays for religious services during the time I enjoyed onboard—and I was the guest pianist!

One month later, we'd made our way to Istanbul, and I was still dying for a decent cup of tea as I bid cheerio to my British friends. "God save the queen and all that" I said, waving to yet another ship disappearing on the horizon, without me.

Standing now on the pier in Istanbul I mouthed towards the vanishing British ship, "No, it's alright mates – I'll just catch a taxi back to Liverpool."

Before I had time to panic, "Merhaba, Lieutenant Bonzo," I heard with a start.

"Jeepers, Toto, that doesn't sound like we're in Kansas, let alone England," I joked nervously with myself. I had been reassigned to the Turkish Navy, which, like Great Britain, had an exchange agreement with the U.S.

Now understand, I had an affinity for languages, but Tyrktfe was not one of them.

The roots of the language can be traced to Central Asia, with the first written records dating back nearly 1,200 years.

To the west, the influence of Ottoman Turkish spread as the Ottoman Empire expanded. In 1928, as one of Ataturk's Reforms in the early years of the Republic of Turkey, the Ottoman script was replaced with a phonetic variation of the Latin alphabet.

Concurrently, the newly founded Turkish Language Association initiated the drive to reform the language by removing Persian and Arabic loanwords in favor of native variants and coinages from Turkic roots.

Huh? I mused walking up the plank onboard another foreign vessel. I wouldn't have a clue what anyone was saying on that ship, but the Turkish sailors wore cute outfits! "Someone on this boat knew how to sew" I thought from behind my steely eyes.

"Allahaismarladik" I said, hoping it meant farewell and nothing to do with their mother or sister, while waving my *right* hand at them, and walking down the gangplank a month later.

I was once again on the pier, yep – alone. At least the Turks had the decency to return me to a nearby taxi stand.

"Next?" I thought. "Now serving foreign navy number three," I continued.

"Just how many countries *are* there in the Old World? Should I have packed less?" I questioned myself.

I continued rambling to no one in sight except a drooling camel with bad breath. His single hump told me I was in Western Asia, and hadn't been deposited to the east in Mongolia or Borneo.

"Let's go, people, who's next? I haven't got all day,"

In fact I had thirty days: I was now on shore leave!

"I've been knighted by the Queen?"

CHAPTER FOURTEEN:
My European Vacation!

"I wonder if I'll meet Clark Griswold," I hummed as I started down my holiday road at Sirkeci Station, Istanbul, which is located in the old heart of the city.

Istanbul straddles two very different continents, just as I was straddling two very different identities, that of the sailor for the U.S. Navy and that of a gay man.

I was relieved to now have a month to myself; even if I still didn't act on my feelings by trying to find Monsieur Droit or Senor Derecha, I could enjoy being more myself on my own on shore leave.

Pausing for a stiff, bracing espresso, I could see before me, arms stretched and skirts billowing out, six men and women spinning and spinning and spinning like tops, part of a ritualistic prayer performed three times a week at the station by a mystic Islamic sect known as the Mevlevi order.

I could see tourists from around the world watching these Whirling Dervishes, watching them intently as the rays of the setting sun pierced through stained glass windows set high in the dome of the station's entrance hall. Vibrant music and dance really suited the station, I decided pleasurably, just as it did on the Turkish warship I had been briefly assigned to.

Outside the station, a nearby dock buzzed with people and taxis awaiting a ferry that would take them across the Bosporus Straight. I dared myself to try speaking Tyrktfe to one of the taxi drivers, but afraid of committing a verbal faus pax that could potentially land me in an Islamic prison; I opted to walk to the relative safety of a hotel room in the British sector of town for one night.

As I threw myself down on the bed, I tried to remember some of the Islamic etiquette I had been taught by the military; don't use your left hand...don't display the sole of you feet...no public displays of affection – huh, no problem there, since I liked men and the military had already deemed that one as conduct unbecoming! Bouncing up from the bed I wondered if the TV worked.

"On star date 3025.3, the starship USS *Enterprise*, under the command of Captain James T. Kirk, arrives at a planet in the Omicron Delta system," said the narrator for this fantasy TV episode I was watching on a flickering screen, in my walk-up hotel room in Istanbul, planet Earth.

"Scans reveal the planet to be congenial, and Kirk announces shore leave for all off-duty personnel." I heard with my left ear, while my right ear tried to determine if the knocking sound was the broken refrigerator compressor, or more worrisome someone at the door.

Turning back towards the TV, it was revealed that the planet Kirk and his crew had chosen for shore leave was a sophisticated amusement park, run by a Caretaker. Their every wish was his job to create for them. "I want a lifetime pass," I pleaded with the TV screen, ignoring the persistent knocking sound in my room.

During my entire shore leave, I would not have sex with another man. Of course, the major reason was that I was afraid the military with its tentacles would find out, and it wasn't worth losing my career for just sex.

Some civilians may find this hard to understand, but for many in the service, being in the military isn't a punishment; it's a career choice.

For me, I loved everything about my work: the feeling that I was serving my country with pride, the work itself, steaming around the world's oceans, and the camaraderie with my fellow sailors. There was no way I was going to forsake all that for a night of pleasure with some stranger.

What's more, I wanted the whole package with another man including love, romance, sex, or just the simple freedom to play with my man's toes in the sand at the beach. That would be my wish, if I were in Kirk's crew, in the Omicron Delta system.

I looked out of the window of the lonely hotel room in Istanbul, towards the sky and wistfully hoped it wouldn't take until the twenty third century, or an imaginary Caretaker for my wish to come true.

Since the knocking sound in my room had finally stopped, I laid down for a nap, almost glad the refrigerator had committed suicide, taking my leftover Adana kebab on pide flatbread with it.

My uncle had also been a sailor, Naval Aviation. Closing my eyes, I remembered the following true story about his shore leave:

"Our ship was directed to the island of Ulithi, South Pacific, having been involved at most of the landings, i.e. Okinawa, Iwo Jima. Our visit was for R& R. The captain went ashore on ship's business and when he returned he called the Mate to his cabin," my uncle had paused his story for a shot of whiskey, which I had declined earning his scrutiny.

Lubricated he continued speaking through his teeth "The Captain said to the Mate that he had planned to grant shore leave, but when ashore he had seen all the women were bare-breasted. He said this would distract his crew, and the Mate was sent ashore with cases of T-shirts. These were given out to all the native women to be worn at all times," my uncle chuckled, or was he just choking on the ozone layer killing cigar he was now enjoying, blowing plumes of smoke in the air like a wood burning, rail-road locomotive.

"The sailors went ashore the next day only to find the women wore the T-shirts, but they had cut two holes where it exposed their breasts. This was to the delight of the sailors. The captain was furious but still allowed leave. It was the talk of the ship," he finished with happy reflection.

Now years hence, remembering my uncle's story as I continued my shore leave, I woke with alarm, looked out the window in every direction frightfully to ensure I hadn't been transported to the same island!

What's more, land just didn't feel right to my sea legs, and I wasn't quite sure what was on the other side of the Bosporus Straight. So, I took the Orient Express in the opposite direction, where I felt I could communicate in a language other than signing.

My private cabin on this elegant train from another era was adjacent to that of a formidable British aristocrat. My humor cracked her armor as decisively as Lord Nelson's fleet had broken through the combined French and Spanish fleets in the Battle of Trafalgar.

We became inseparable friends throughout much of Europe. I sensed she knew I was gay, yet tactfully overlooked it. If only the United States military would do the same!

We were taken by train from Istanbul, to Greece, then Italy, France, and England with stops and side trips along the way. Once in Her Majesty's realm we would part graciously, but not before one last episode.

We disembarked at Victoria Station. With the British Pullman cars of the Wagons-Lits as a back drop, she walked slowly towards her awaiting stretched Jaguar motor car. I kept pace, having been invited to do so, and relished the informality. "Do you like Shakespeare," she asked without changing her forward motion or gaze.

"Yes, quite," I responded eagerly, realizing in an instant that in "British" English *quite* means *not really*.

A slight smile on her face, and a slight tilt of her head towards me indicated she understood and forgave my American use of the English language.

"Romeo, Romeo, wherefore art thou Romeo. Deny thy father and refuse thy name, or thou wilt not, be but sworn my love..." she spoke with a passion I envied.

"Act two, scene one?" I questioned her, already knowing I was right. I also understood where she was going with the dialogue, as *wherefore* means not where, but *why* in the play. Juliet is asking Romeo to resolve the tension between his social, family identity, and his inner identity –something I had been secretly trying to do since boot camp, and with ever increasing frustration.

Reaching her awaiting car, its door already opened by a uniformed valet, she paused, and turned to face me. I felt the crispness of both her white gloves as she took my hand, and then simply smiled.

It's often what is *not* said, that also speaks Shakespearean-like volumes.

She went wherever persons of her class go, with *all* of her Louis Vuitton luggage, and I decided to have a look about London, then head back towards continental Europe with my one, old duffle bag.

No wonder there were British expats everywhere I went in the world; they were trying to escape English weather, I thought immediately upon exiting the railway station, looking up at grey, wet skies.

The great Russian poet of the 19th century, Aleksander Pushkin, had written in one of his poems: "Oh, summer, beautiful, I would have loved you most, if not the scorching heat…"

Hum, perhaps I should have gone to Russia!

Upon reaching Regents Park, which had a fantastic landscape designed by renowned architect John Nash and the largest outdoor sports area in London, I discovered row upon row of wooden chairs, still folded away and waiting too for a ray of sunshine to invite them to open up.

I had just walked through the famed London Zoo next door and needed a rest before going back to the train station. As soon as I unfolded one chair from the front row and sat back leisurely, voila! The sun came out! Good thing, too; it would kill the mold I was certain was growing on me after only one day in this wet gloom.

I closed my eyes and was taking in the ten minutes of annual sunshine in the British Isles, when a pointed object began taping me on the shoulder.

"I've been knighted by the Queen?" I imagined, opening my eyes humbly.

Not quite, but it was a proper English Gentleman with a proper British brollie who spoke to me from a great height above his nose "I say, may we have two chairs, my lad?"

"Right oh, guv" I played along. "There we go, my lord" I continued the charade with a convincing East-end London, working class accent, as I set up and wiped clean two chairs.

Subsequently I took a taxi to the train station with the five pound note I had just earned in gratuity from his lordship. If the military ever threw me out for being gay, I could just hand out chairs in the park.

Having changed trains to the high-speed TGV and now zooming towards hopefully warmer, drier weather on the continent, I discovered abruptly that my assigned dining companion was a blond-haired, blue-eyed handsome young man from France.

He clicked his heels before sitting at our table in the dining car. He rarely spoke, except to command the salt and pepper from my side of the table, which I obediently supplied as quickly as the English had beaten the French at the Battle of Agincourt.

Anecdotal, as that was the battle where raising the middle finger began its assembly into pop culture as an act of defiance.

The French had boasted they were going to kick the British arses, and after the battle would cut off all the Brits bow-fingers, rendering them unable to use their bows in battle again. Well, as I said, the British won at Agincourt and as an act of defiance towards the French raised their intact middle "bow" fingers into the air.

I had resisted the gesture during my archery classes at University having scored above my classmates, and now in the dining car on the TGV. Some forms of communication just didn't translate well into modern lingo.

It was curious that he was so aloof. Was he straight? Or was he gay, and afraid of being found out, like me? No matter; I shrugged and decided not to pursue him, however cute and well-manicured he was, while motioning in the air to the *garcon* for more wine.

The TGV whisked me hurriedly on the remainder of my shore leave (just as well, since now no one was talking to me and good wine wasn't cheap) and at a more modern pace from Normandy to Southern France, connecting to Switzerland, Italy, and West Germany.

Among all, it was the interpersonal relationships, albeit fleeting and at times unrequited, that I enjoyed the most. To listen was to learn, and to understand would be to inspire.

My European vacation had been done in just under thirty days. I had joined the Navy to, among other things, see the world and boy did I.

Yet, because of the very fact I was in the military service, an enduring relationship was out of the question.

"Now who's rushing?" I asked myself at Rhein-Main air base, panting over a latte, waiting for the trip back to the States, back to the real, familiar world of the U.S. military.

Rhein-Main Air Base is a small base named after the confluence of the Rheine and Main (pronounced mine) rivers located to the west of Frankfurt.

I sat down wearily on a wooden slat bench inside the hanger which in 1909, Count von

Zeppelin had used as a landing site for his lighter-than-air dirigible Z-II.

Easing my head onto my sweater turned pillow and nodding off; I hoped the military wasn't going to send me to my next duty station on a balloon full of explosive gas.

I felt like I had been running away: but from what and from whom? I wondered how long I'd have to continue to hide, and wondered where I'd be going next. Would I ever meet someone special, or for that matter be *allowed* to? My mind fatigued, my eyes finally closed.

Pushkin had also written "I have lived to burry my desires, and see my dreams corrode with rust." "Ya soglasen," I nodded affirmatively in my sleep.

Previously, during my shore leave, I had called my Detailer, and asked what my next assignment would be.

Over the phone line, I heard pages of potential venues being shuffled through. "Alaska?" he barked into the phone in a voice that was vaguely familiar to me.

"Too cold," I said tersely.

"NAS Belle Chasse?" he said with affected pride in his voice.

"Too hot," I said, acting out *Goldilocks and the Three Bears*.

"Damn it, isn't there any sea duty available?" I asked pleadingly. "Put me on a nice aircraft carrier or cruiser?" I continued. "Even assign me to a vintage PT boat? I'll take anything that floats!" I cried, losing steam.

"OK" he said with a sneer, "I've got it: You're going to New Zealand, Lieutenant Bon-zai."

Now, I woke with a jolt on the hard bench in the Zeppelin hanger, looked down at my orders and confirmed that they indeed said Auckland, not Oakland. I was being assigned to Operation Deep Freeze, a "research" mission to Antarctica.

Here we go again, I thought, another "research" mission. What, were we planning to invade an iceberg now? How many Seals would it take to beat up on a bunch of penguins? They are flightless – it wouldn't be much of a challenge!

Grabbing my bag, I scurried towards the tarmac wondering if they served lunch on this MAC (Military Airlift Command) flight.

"It's time to look to the future, and not look back," I wrote, taking my turn with less than eloquent graffiti on the grey steel inner skin of the transport plane. "To live each day as if it were my last" I finished the simple, but profound truth.

En-route to being stationed in Christchurch, New Zealand, where our base of "research" operations to Antarctica was located, I resolved during the long hours of the flight that I would end my long years of running and hiding. My growing doubt regarding being able to serve my country, as a gay man, was the beginning of wisdom.

I would resign my active duty commission.

My knees weren't shaking.

I would quit and it would be over, just like that.

"What do you do when you have no tears left?"

Don't Ask, Do Tell

CHAPTER FIFTEEN: DOR:

From: Secretary of the Navy

To: Lt. William J. Bonzo, SC, USN

Via: CO, Naval Personnel Center

Subj: Acceptance of resignation

Ref: (a) Your resignation

Encl: (1) Honorable discharge certificate

1. In accordance with your request contained in reference (a), and by the direction of the President, your resignation from the U.S. Navy is hereby accepted under honorable condition effective immediately.

2. The Navy Department at this time expresses its appreciation of your past services and trusts that you will continue your interest in the naval service.

SECRETARY OF THE NAVY

Yeah, it looked like a "confirmed kill" by the Navy: DOR, Dead on Request.

It had been a personal tug of war.

What was I to do when I had no tears left?

I had asked myself what had I been fighting for, and had it been worth risking my life for? My immediate response was, "My country, and absolutely!"

Was it worth having to wear metaphorical camouflage every day in order to hide my sexual orientation? Was it worth feeling love and knowing that love was forbidden? Was it worth living a lie, always being afraid of my true self being found out?

I considered this question for a long time—perhaps, in some ways I was considering it for years before I resigned.

Finally, I concluded with humility that innumerable others have paid a much higher price while serving our country in uniform. I was lucky; I came back alive, and not physically injured. But the wounds to my psyche, and the wounds suffered by every other gay man and lesbian in the military, are real and long-lasting.

I don't regret serving, not for a minute. And yet my anger and hurt at the military's policy remain with me every day.

"Kiss my gay ass!"

Don't Ask, Do Tell

THE END

"What? That's the end?" you ask, slamming this book you were just reading down, and walking away from it smoldering.

Yes, it is, because that is just as abrupt and frustrated as I felt when my military career had come to an end.

You want more? So did I.

Am I angry? Damn right, I am – but not at you.

It's the military who can kiss my gay ass!

EPILOGUE

It's been years since I resigned my Navy commission and left active military duty. I'm now in Hawaii taking care of my properties.

Having been humid recently, one of my tenants asked me in the middle of the night for an air conditioner. I slid open his lanai doors, informed him that the trade winds would be back by that afternoon and asked with residual military formality "Is there anything else I can do for you?"

After taking care of business, I always settle quickly into my island routine: up at the crack of dawn, Kona coffee, fresh fruit and listening to the arguments of my neighbors while sitting on my lanai. Honestly, those two birds need to decide who's gonna fly and get breakfast, and who's gonna stay and watch the kids in the nest.

I volunteered to watch the kids. One of the adult birds, with whom I had been engaged in conversation on my lanai, shook their head quickly left and right disapprovingly, and then flew away from my lanai with my croissant in its beak! "You forgot the guava jelly," I mouthed towards the banyan tree that is their home. "Well, at least with your mouths full I'll get some peace and quiet" I continued, smiling, now looking vaguely towards the familiar yacht harbor. It's just as well my neighbors didn't take the guava jelly too, cause guava acts like Draino—be right back...

Once again in my own comfortable perch, I see a nice rainbow just off my lanai, framing the masts of the yachts and in the distance a Navy Cruiser is sailing out of Pearl Harbor. I wish I was going with them, going to...

The unmistakable roar of a Harley Davidson jolts me from my nostalgia, and I know my Marine Corps buddy has come to get me and my new Harley VROD to go to the beach with him on the North Shore of Oahu. "Eh brah, like go beach, or what?" he says in Hawaiian Pidgin English that always makes me smile, along with how he lets *himself* into my house.

I jump at the idea, even though not fully recovered from our previous fun–filled evening at the annual military carnival on Kaneohe Marine Corps base; on base, when among other people, he insists we walk at least two feet apart!

"Let's scare Jesus out of a few tourists with our bikes, on the way," I shout at him over the patented misfire of their v-twin engines. We wrap our legs around the throbbing machines, smile at each other, steer mauka and enjoy the freedom of riding side by side over the Pali Highway, and through the majestic Ko'olau mountain range that divides the island into Leeward, and less populous Windward halves.

Picking a spot at remote Bellows Air Force Station beach in the Ko'olaupoko District, meaning "short windward," or to us "the most secluded," we strip down to just board-shorts. After an invigorating swim, our wet shorts clinging to our bodies, we sit close to each other at water's edge.

The palm trees swaying in the trade winds are the only other activity here today, no tourists, and many of the island's military compliment are serving in either Iraq or Afghanistan.

"The USS *Honolulu* is back in port at Pearl," he says, making small talk, and referring to our capital's namesake, one of the Navy's newest Los Angeles class attack submarines SSN-718.

"Yea, I know," I reply in a wistful tone. "One of my friends, Lieutenant Gandy, is the navigator onboard. His wife Jenna and I have been waiting for him for over six months, on pins-and-needles, to get back alive from the Persian Gulf. We're like two women on a Widow's Walk at her Penthouse unit at the Mauna Luan in Hawaii Kai."

He laughs in response and quips "That's not the same moron navigator from boot-camp you told me about, is it?"

"Nah – Hey, the ship's motto is *Maka Ala Mau*; know what it means?" I challenge him, skimming a rock and getting three jumps with it on the surface of the unusually calm water in front of us.

"It's Hawaiian for *Always on Alert, brah*" he replies quickly, while throwing his rock makai and getting a four jump with it.

A heavenly amount of time passes just being alone with him. I shake the water out of my now shoulder-length blond hair like a wet dog. He tries to imitate me, amusing since he has a *snatch patch* – Marine haircut. Our toes are playing with each other's in the sand when he asks "Do you miss it, you know, the military?"

I look first out to sea, then down at our entwined toes, and finally into his handsome green eyes and answer him painfully. "Even though I am highly decorated, and with only top marks on my Fitness Reports, one persistent comment by all my Commanding officers and which probably contributed to my resignation and final discharge, was *William can be aloof, at times.*

"Gee, d'ya think!" I respond in the air to all my previous commanders. "Stop persecuting gays and lesbians in the military and we'll turn into the kind of person I am now: open, honest, and engaging."

I feel his arms around me, and enjoy the simple embrace, but worry for him since he is on active military duty and still living the lie.

Aloha nui loa,

William Bonzo,

ACKNOWLEDGMENTS

To the Vdara in Las Vegas, my writing refuge, thanks for the soaking tub, and especially for the delectable in-room dining!

Bev, your support and laughter while reading the rough drafts told me I was on track.

To Sweet Inspirations in The Castro, thanks for my window seat on the gay world, which is a constant reminder that it's OK to be me, and I'm *sorry* about the car alarms! I'll put the baffles back on my Harley.

Steven, you always smell good.

Takahiro, thanks for the first-class tickets on United Airlines. I'm just too damned big to sit in economy!

Theresa, Anne and Sarah, thanks for the technical support.

Silvia, I always enjoy your warm hugs, but if you don't stop jaywalking across Market Street, you're gonna get killed!

And most importantly, all the servicemen and women who risk their lives every day, which allows me the freedom to write this book.

Who is This Guy?

Just visit me online at www.dontaskdotellonline. com.

You'll have the opportunity to see more pictures of me, listen to some of my favorite music, and even read other's comments, or leave one of your own!

AFTERWORD

Hey! You the opponents of allowing gay men and lesbian women to serve in the armed forces; go sit in your closet, *go now!* I'll wait...

Now, you just stay in there—*no peeking out either!* Remember, I am an Expert with small weapons. Yea, you just stay in that closet until Congress says you can come out and play with all the other, *normal* boys and girls. Uh huh, that's what I thought—you don't wanna play anymore either, do ya? *Now* you know what it is like for every gay and lesbian serving our country in uniform.

"But the House has repealed Don't Ask, Don't Tell" you say.

No, my dears, they approved a "proposal" to repeal the policy, not the actual policy. What's more, the proposal to repeal Don't Ask, Don't Tell faces a tough fight in the Senate *and* hinges on a military review. "It would repeal Don't Ask, Don't Tell only after, and I repeat after, the ongoing high-level review is completed" said United States Secretary of Defense.

What's more, the conservative Family Research Council said on May 26, 2010 that "A repeal of DADT will lead to soldiers having unwanted gay sex..." and "the repeal would pave the way for a free-rape zone."

"A Federal judge has ruled in September, 2010 that Don't Ask' Don't Tell is unconstitutional," you persist.

Yes, and I'm proud of your knowledge of social events. However, another Federal judge months before ruled that Proposition 8 is unconstitutional – yet same-sex couples *still* can't get married!

Also, yet lesser known, in September of 2010 Fidel Castro, a big man who has influenced all our lives, acknowledged that the Cuban model of Soviet-style Communism "doesn't work for us anymore."

Who would 'a thunk?

His words give me strength, knowing that we can continue to change, and grow in understanding.

I ask you my readers to accept change too, embrace it, nurture it, and be a bigger person yourself by supporting gay men and lesbian women serving openly in the United States armed forces.

That too would give me strength, so I can remember that I fought, and that gay men and lesbian women continue to fight, so that persons have the right to freedom, including freedom of speech.

However much I as fervently believe many are full of *shit*.

www.ingramcontent.com/pod-product-compliance
Lightning Source LLC
Chambersburg PA
CBHW062203280526
45788CB00001B/421